THE ROYAL NAVY IN 1980-89

1980-89

F 88

Steve Bush

First published in the United Kingdom in 2012 by Maritime Books, Lodge Hill, Liskeard, Cornwall, PL14 4EL

AUTHOR'S NOTES

When compiling a volume such as this, it is always good to bear in mind your potential customer. A large percentage of those who buy this book will be former sailors, who at some time during the 1980s spent a part of their career in one of these fine ships. From the outset then, I feel that I have to make an apology. In order to produce a commercially viable book it is not possible to include a photograph of every ship that was in service throughout the decade. There were over 320 ships sailing under the white ensign of the Royal Navy or the blue ensign of the Royal Fleet Auxiliary. I have tried to ensure that there is a reasonable spread of images and, with a few exceptions, there is an example of most of the major vessels from the period.

Another apology is due to all XOs and Buffers who take so much pride in the appearance of their ships. I have on, the whole tried to use pictures which show the vessels off at their best but, while not wanting this to be a Falklands book, I couldn't ignore the significance of that conflict and there are a couple of images which show ships in a less than flattering light. But rather than being a slight to the professionalism of those whose job it is to keep HM Ships in good outward appearance, it goes to show the realities of operating warships and auxiliaries in a harsh maritime environment for prolonged periods some 8,000 miles away from the nearest UK Naval Base. That many of the ships within these pages did just that is a testimony to the professionalism of their respective ship's companies.

Finally, credit must be given to the many Royal Navy photographers whose images appear within this book. It is through their hard work and skill that the Royal Navy and its ships are brought to life on operations around the World - in conditions ranging from the sun-kissed tropical waters of the Caribbean to the harsh winter conditions of the South Atlantic during combat operations. It is their work that enables us, the public, to see the Royal Navy at work.

Dedicated to the men and women of Operation Corporate
who, in 1982, sailed to the South Atlantic to drive
an occupying force from the Falkland Islands
and in memoriam to those who failed to return.

INTRODUCTION

As the Royal Navy sailed into the 1980s it had already said goodbye to conventional fixed-wing carrier strike with the de-commissioning of HMS ARK ROYAL and, as a result, the loss of her Phantom, Buccaneer and Gannet aircraft. The last of the cruisers TIGER and BLAKE were now consigned to history and the noises coming from within Government were not painting a very bright future for the Royal Navy.

The country was in recession and the Cold War was at its peak. In 1981 the infamous John Nott Defence Review proposed that the RN would never operate as anything other than an arm of NATO and that therefore, it should be shaped to provide a specialist anti-submarine warfare capability to defend the North Atlantic against possible Soviet incursion. It was thought that the RN would never have to operate out of area again, and that the bulk of its new capability could be achieved through the use of nuclear-powered submarines and a small force of specialist ASW surface ships. A smaller number of frigates and coastal craft would be maintained for constabulary duties.

Future warship programmes, such as the Type 43 and Type 44 destroyers were cancelled, as was development of Sea Dart II. It was proposed to close Chatham Naval Base, and the recently delivered aircraft carrier INVINCIBLE was to be offered for sale to Australia. With the requirement to operate out of area no longer an issue, the Royal Marines and Amphibious War-fare were to be hit particularly hard, with the entire Corps in jeopardy of being axed, and as a consequence, the amphibious assault ships FEARLESS and INTREPID being placed on the disposal list. Another cut was to be the sole Ice Patrol Ship, ENDURANCE, which spent six months of the year in the Antarctic supporting the British Antarctic Survey and maintaining a presence around UK interests in the South Atlantic.

It was, perhaps, the decision to withdraw ENDURANCE which signalled a reprieve for the RN, as that single act was seen by the military Junta in Argentina as a signal that the UK was not interested in the South Atlantic and so encouraged them to initiate the invasion of South Georgia and the Falkland Islands and so begin a chain of events that would see the UK en-gaged in combat 8000 miles away from home on a remote set of islands in the South Atlantic.

When the call came in April 1982, the RN was in a position to rapidly deploy as sizeable force of ships to the area, as a large fleet had been assembled in the Mediterranean for exercise Springtrain. The larger ships, aircraft carriers, amphibious ships and their escorts followed from the UK all rapidly stored, upgraded, enhanced and repaired, by dockyard workers which had been engaged in industrial dispute and working to rule. Ships weree quickly taken up from trade and fitted with flight decks, refuelling equipment and naval communications. Liners were converted to hospital and troopships, civilian tankers given facilities to pump fuel direct into waiting RFAs and fishing trawlers converted into minesweepers. The arnmed forces and the civilian support staff, be they in MoD or the naval bases rose to the challenge and delivered whatever was required.

Fortunately, many of the proposed cuts of the 1981 defence review had not yet taken effect and ships which were due to be sold, decommissioned or placed in reserve, were quickly reprieved and brought back up to full service, including INVINCI-BLE, which proved essential over the coming months. HERMES was just emerging from refit and was fully sored and made ready to sail. INTREPID was brought out of reserve ain record time.

The battle over the Falklands was as quick as it was bloody and by June the Falklands were back in UK hands. The cost in men and ships had been grave. SHEFFIELD, COVENTRY, ARDENT and AMBUSCADE had been sunk. SIR GALAHAD had been so badly damaged that she was sunk after the war. The list of damaged ships was long and it was only due to the fact that the Argentine bombs on many occasions failed to detonate, that the loss of ships was not greater.

Many lessons were learnt from the Falklands experience - not least among the politicians who realised the folly of the 1981 Defence Review. The RN, and the military in general were enjoying a hitherto unknown popularity among the UK public and before long, the RN was experiencing a build up in capability not seen, and probably not dreamt of, in many years.

The immediate consequence of the Falklands was the realisation at how susceptible our ships were to air attack in confined waters and the dangers from within once damage had occurred. The small calibre weapons on most ships was increased, with improved batteries of 30mm and 20mm being added - some used WWII vintage 20mm Oerlikons, others brand new 20mm Bmarc or twin 30mm Gambo mountings. For the larger vessels, 20mm Vulcan Phalanx CIWS were acquired. Internally the ships were fitted with smoke curtains to help stem the spread of smoke once fire had taken hold. Toxic materials in furnishings and cable runs were replaced and cables left unpainted. Shatterproof bulkhead coverings were adopted and aluminium was removed from all structural areas of new build warships.

The older Type 12, Leander and Type 21 class frigates were to be replaced by a new class of Type 22 ASW frigate, gas turbine powered and much larger than their older steam powered forbears, the boasted advanced missile systems, electronics and increased helicopter carrying capability. It was intended to maintain a destroyer frigate force of around 50 ships, but this would prove difficult as the newer warships, being so sophisticated were very expensive. As a consequence, the Leander class frigates, in their various guises as Ikara, Exocet or Seawolf conversions, soldiered on well into the next decade.

The requirement to keep a significant presence in the South Atlantic saw the older Type 12 and Tribal class frigates running on longer than expected to try to fill the voids - the RN still had to fulfill its standard commitments ranging from West Indies

Guardship; Standing Naval Force Atlantic; Standing Naval Force Mediterranean; Hong Kong Guardship as well as contingency roles around the UK.

The MCM and patrol forces were also heavily employed, patrolling offshore oil and gas installations, fishery protection duties and anti-terror patrols off Northern Ireland in an effort to stem arms-smuggling to the IRA. The MCM force, which for many years comprised the ubiquitous Ton class Coastal Minesweepers, was slowly being replaced by a new generation of GRP hulled ships. Both the Hunt and the Sandown class were beginning to enter service and a new class of 12 steel-hulled River class were purchased to provide at sea training for the RNR.

As the decade drew to a close, the first of the new generation Type 23 frigates was undergoing sea trials ready to be handed over in 1990 just as the last of the Batch III Type 22 frigate was under construction. A new class of conventional diesel powered submarine was close to entering service and the remaining Trafalgar class nuclear-powered submarines was under construction.

By the end of the 1980s the outlook for the RN was much better than it was at the beginning of the decade - it had taken a war, the loss of ships and many brave sailors, to turn things around - but finally, the true value of a properly funded, properly equipped RN was being realised.

Steve Bush
Plymouth
2012

GLOSSARY

AA	Anti-aircraft
AAW	Anti-air Warfare
AEW	Air Early Warning
AS	Anti-submarine
ASW	Anti-submarine Warfare
AUWE	Admiralty Underwater Weapons Establishment
CIWS	Close-In Weapon System
CMS	Coastal Minesweeper
DML	Devonport Management Limited
DS	Destroyer Squadron
DTS	Dartmouth Training Squadron
EDATS	Extra Deep Armed Team Sweep
EOD	Explosive Ordnance Disposal
ESM	Electronic Support Measures
FOST	Flag Officer Sea Training
FPS	Fishery Protection Squadron
FS	Frigate Squadron
FTB	Fast Training Boat
GIUK	Greenland, Iceland, UK
GPMG	General Purpose Machine Gun
GRP	Glass Re-inforced Plastic
GWS	Guided Weapon System
HKPS	Hong Kong Patrol Squadron
HMAFV	Her Majesty's Air Force Vessel
HMSML	Her Majesty's Survey Motor Launch
ICGV	Icelandic Coast Guard Vessel
IHTU	Inter-service Hovercraft Trials Unit
IMS	Inshore Minesweeper
LSL	Landing Ships Logistic
LST	Landing Ship (Tank)
MCMS	Mie Counter Measures Squadron
MCMV	Mine Counter Measures Vessel
MSC	Military Sealift Command
MSS	Mine Sweeping Squadron
MV	Merchant Vessel
NAS	Naval Air Squadron
NATO	North Atlantic Treaty Organisation
NGS	Naval Gunfire Support
NHTU	Naval Hovercraft Trials Unit
PBS	Patrol Boat Squadron
PCRS	Primary Casualty Receiving Ship
PNS	Pakistan Navy Ship
RNR	Royal Naval Reserve
RNVR	Royal Naval Volunteer Reserve
RNXS	Royal Naval Auxiliary Service
RTTL	Rescue and Target Towing Launch
SDSR	Strategic Defence & Security Review
SFPA	Scottish Fishery Protection Agency
SNFL	Standing Naval Force Atlantic
SNMG2	Standing NATO Maritime Group 2
STWS	Shipborne Torpedo Weapon System
TLAM	Tomahawk Land Attack Missile
UAV	Underwater Autonomous Vehicle
URNU	University Royal Naval Unit
USNS	United States Navy Ship
USS	United States Ship
VDS	Variable Depth Sonar
VSEL	Vickers Shipbuilding and Engineering Ltd
XSV	Auxiliary Service Vessel

INDEX OF
ROYAL NAVY & ROYAL FLEET AUXILIARY SHIPS
FROM 1980-89

AIRCRAFT CARRIERS

Bulwark (R08)	1954-1981

Originally employed as a conventional aircraft carrier the ship was converted in 1960 to operate as a Commando Carrier. She paid off in 1976 but was reactivated in 1979 as an ASW carrier to cover for delays in the completion of Invincible. She decommissioned in 1981 and thought was given to reactivating her for the Falklands campaign, but a survey determined that she had deteriorated too much.

Hermes (R12)	1959-1984

The ship was declared to NATO as an ASW carrier but she retained a secondary role as a Commando Carrier with accommodation for a Commando of 750 officers and men.

Invincible Class

Ark Royal (R07)	1985-2011
Illustrious (R06)	1982-Pres

Invincible (R05)	1979-2005

Designed to act as command ships of ASW forces. In addition to Sea King helicopters, they also carry Sea Harrier aircraft and the Sea Dart missile system which enabled them to contribute to air defence and anti-ship operations. Post Falklands they were equipped with Close-in Weapon Systems for self defence.

AMPHIBIOUS SHIPS

Fearless (L10)	1965-2002
Intrepid (L11)	1967-1999

Throughout the period these two ships were the RN's most versatile vessels for amphibious warfare and proved their worth during the Falklands campaign. In addition to their ability convey troops and to move them ashore via their embarked landing craft and assault helicopters, each was fitted out as a Naval Assault Group/Brigade HQ from which naval and military personnel could mount and control an amphibious operation.

SUBMARINES

Resolution Class

Renown (S26)	1968-1995
Repulse (S23)	1968-1996
Resolution (S22)	1967-1994
Revenge (S27)	1969-1992

The four Resolution class submarines carried the UKs strategic nuclear deterrent. At least one submarine was on patrol at anyone time and each carried up to 16 Polaris inter-continental ballistic missiles. To maintain a high tempo of operations each submarine had two crews.

Dreadnought Class

Dreadnought (S101)	1963-1982

The RNs first nuclear-powered submarine,

she was built in the UK, but powered by an American nuclear plant. She was the prototype to the subsequent Valiant class.

Valiant Class

Churchill (S46)	1970-1991
Conqueror (S48)	1971-1990
Courageous (S50)	1971-1992
Valiant (S102)	1966-1994
Warspite (S103)	1967-1990

Five Valiant class Fleet submarines were operated by the RN. Capable of continuous patrols at high underwater speed, the only limit to their endurance was the amount of food that could be carried for the crew.

Swiftsure Class

Sceptre (S104)	1978-2010
Sovereign (S108)	1974-2005
Spartan (S105)	1979-2006
Splendid (S106)	1980-2003
Superb (S109)	1976-2008
Swiftsure (S126)	1973-1992

The six submarines of this class moved away from the traditional tear-drop hull design to one with a more continuous diameter throughout the length of the vessel. They had a reputation for being very quiet submarines. They also had a significant anti-ship capability with the introduction of the Sub-Harpoon missile.

Trafalgar Class

Tireless (S117)	1985-Pres
Torbay (S118)	1987-Pres
Trafalgar (S107)	1983-2009
Trenchant (S91)	1989-2011
Turbulent (S110)	1984-Pres

A development of the Swiftsure class, incorporating quieter technology, this class of fleet submarine would eventually comprise seven vessels. Technology had also moved away from propellers towards shrouded pumpjets.

'P' Class

Porpoise (S01)	1958-1985
Sealion (S07)	1961-1988
Walrus (S08)	1961-1987

The survivors of a class of eight diesel-electric patrol submarines built for the RN from the mid-1950s. Exceptionally quiet boats, each submarine's armament consisted of eight 21-inch torpedo tubes; six in the bow, and two in the stern.

'O' Class

Oberon (S09)	1961-1986
Ocelot (S17)	1964-1991
Odin (S10)	1962-1990
Olympus (S12)	1962-1989
Onslaught (S14)	1962-1990
Onyx (S21)	1967-1990
Opossum (S19)	1964-1993
Opportune (S20)	1964-1992
Oracle (S16)	1963-1993
Orpheus (S11)	1960-1986
Osiris (S13)	1964-1993
Otter (S15)	1962-1991
Otus (S18)	1963-1992

The Oberon class comprised 13 submarines in RN service, although 27 submarines of this class served around the world. Based on the previous Porpoise-class they were constructed of stronger steel thereby giving them a greater diving depth.

DESTROYERS

County Class

Antrim (D18)	1970-1984
Fife (D20)	1966-1987
Glamorgan (D19)	1966-1986
Kent (D12)	1963-1980
London (D16)	1963-1981
Norfolk (D21)	1970-1981

Eight County class destroyers were operated by the RN and of the six that remained during this period, all except London and Kent, had thier second 4.5-inch turret replaced by four Exocet missile launchers. Glamorgan survived an Exocet attack during the Falklands war. The land-launched missile hit her on the port side in the vicinity of the hangar.

Type 82

Bristol (D23)	1972-1991

She was the only Type 82 destroyer to be built. Originally conceived as a class of escorts for the cancelled CVA-01 carrier project Bristol entered service in 1972 as a trials vessel for the Sea Dart and Ikara missile systems. It was not until 1979 that she was fitted out for frontline operations. Due to her size and space she was ideal as a flagship, being able to embark staff and having good command and control facilities. By the end of the 1980s, she was deemed too large and too manpower intensive and her service days were numbered.

Type 42 Batch I & II

Birmingham (D86)	1976-1999
Cardiff (D108)	1979-2005
Coventry (D118)	1978-1982
Exeter (D89)	1980-2009
Glasgow (D88)	1978-2005
Liverpool (D92)	1982-2012
Newcastle (D87)	1978-2005
Nottingham (D91)	1982-2010
Sheffield (D80)	1974-1982
Southampton (D90)	1981-2009

Ten of these so called 'stumpy Type 42's were completed, their main role being that of air defence, for which they were equipped with the Sea Dart missile system. Early ships were equipped with the Type 965 radar, but later units received the more modern Type 1022 (later backfitted to the remainder of the class). Two of the class, Sheffield and Coventry, were lost during the Falklands War.

Type 42 Batch III

Edinburgh (D97)	1985-Pres
Gloucester (D96)	1985-2011
Manchester (D95)	1982-2011
York (D98)	1985-Pres

These four ships were a stretched version of the earlier class being some 40ft longer. Post Falklands War all were fitted with Close in Weapon Systems for self protection, but their limited internal space meant that, throughout their careers, the ships were unable to be modernised to any significant extent and later in their careers strengthening beams had to be added to the hulls.

FRIGATES

Type 12 Whitby Class

Torquay (F43)	1956-1985

The sole remaining operational example of the six strong Type 12 Whitby class. Similar to the Rothesay class below, these older ships were never modernised to operate a helicopter. A sister ship, Eastbourne, remained in service as a static harbour training ship.

Type 12 Rothesay Class

Berwick (F115)	1961-1985
Brighton (F106)	1961-1981
Falmouth (F113)	1961-1984
Londonderry (F108)	1960-1984
Lowestoft (F103)	1961-1985
Plymouth (F126)	1961-1987
Rhyl (F129)	1960-1983
Rothesay (F107)	1960-1987
Yarmouth (F101)	1960-1986

The Type 12 frigates were designed to counter the growing Soviet submarine threat. Their primary ASW weapon were two triple-barrelled Limbo AS Mortars. They were all modernised to operate a Wasp helicopter and had a Seacat missile system installed on the hangar roof. A set of Limbo mortars was sacrificed to allow for the provision of a flight deck.

Type 81 Tribal Class

Ashanti (F117)	1961-1981
Eskimo (F119)	1963-1981
Gurkha (F122)	1963-1984
Mohawk (F125)	1963-1981
Nubian (F131)	1962-1981
Tartar (F131)	1962-1984
Zulu (F124)	1964-1984

Designed as General Purpose frigates, their steam machinery was supplemented by gas turbines to boost their speed and enable them to leave harbour at short notice. Most had begun to enter the Standby Squadron by the start of the decade. However, the advent of the Falklands War, and the need for escorts to replace those deployed to the South Atlantic, and those returning damaged, saw three reactivated.

Leander Class

Achilles (F12)	1970-1989
Ajax (F114)	1963-1985
Andromeda (F57)	1968-1993
Apollo (F70)	1972-1988
Arethusa (F38)	1965-1989
Argonaut (F56)	1967-1993
Ariadne (F72)	1972-1992
Aurora (F10)	1964-1987
Bacchante (F69)	1969-1982
Charybdis (F75)	1969-1991
Cleopatra (F28)	1966-1992
Danae (F47)	1967-1991
Dido (F104)	1963-1983
Diomede (F16)	1971-1988
Euryalus (F15)	1964-1989
Galatea (F18)	1964-1986
Hermione (F58)	1969-1992
Juno (F52)	1967-1992
Jupiter (F60)	1969-1993
Leander (F109)	1963-1986
Minerva (F45)	1966-1992
Naiad (F39)	1965-1988

Phoebe (F42)	1966-1990
Penelope (F127)	1963-1991
Scylla (F71)	1970-1993
Sirius (F40)	1966-1993

The Leander class frigates, numbering 26 vessels, was the largest class of frigate to be built for the RN since WWII. They were originally conceived as General Purpose frigates, with a significant ASW capability. As a result of extensive modernisation, eight of the class were refitted to carry the Ikara missile system, while a further eight were modernised to carry the Exocet missile system. The remaining ships were to be modernised to carry both the Exocet and Seawolf missiles, though in the end only five were converted. A handful of the Exocet Leanders were further converted to carry a Towed Array sonar system.

Type 21

Active (F171)	1977-1994
Alacrity (F174)	1977-1994
Amazon (F169)	1974-1993
Ambuscade (F172)	1975-1993
Antelope (F170)	1975-1982
Ardent (F184)	1977-1982
Arrow (F173)	1976-1994
Avenger (F185)	1978-1994

General purpose frigates designed by Vosper, they were armed with a 4.5-inch Mk8 gun, Seacat missiles and a Wasp helicopter. In later service they received the Exocet missile system and operated the Lynx helicopter. All were powered by gas turbines, Olympus for high speeds and Tynes for cruising. They were constructing with the extensive use of aluminium in the superstructure, which subsequently was found to be very poor once subject to battle damage, particularly to fire. Both Antelope and Ardent were lost during the Falklands War of 1982.

Type 22 Batch I

Battleaxe (F89)	1980-1997
Broadsword (F88)	1979-1995
Brazen (F91)	1982-1994
Brilliant (F90)	1981-1996

Designed for the ASW role, these ships represented a number of firsts for the RN, being the first designed from the outset with a missile main armament and no large gun. In addition they were the first to be designed to metric standards. The ships were armed with four Exocet missiles for anti-ship strike and two sextuple launchers for the Seawolf, anti-air missile system.

Type 22 Batch II

Boxer (F92)	1984-1999
Beaver (F93)	1984-1999
Brave (F94)	1986-1999
London (F95)	1987-1999

| Sheffield (F96) | 1988-2002 |
| Coventry (F98) | 1988-2002 |

This second batch of Type 22 frigates were laid down after the Falklands war and incorporated many of the lessons learned, including a minimum of aluminium structure, shatterproof wall coverings, non-toxic cabling and the use of smoke-curtains to slow-down the spread of smoke during a fire. The ships were stretched but their armament was the same as the earlier Batch. However, the flight deck and hangar were extended, starting with Brave, to enable Sea King helicopters to be operated.

Type 22 Batch III

Cornwall (F99)	1988-2011
Cumberland (F85)	1989-2011
Campbeltown (F86)	1989-2011

The final Batch III ships would comprise four vessels (Chatham being commissioned in 1990). They differed in having a 4.5-inch gun introduced on the forecastle and the Exocet being replace by two quadruple Harpoon launchers sited aft of the bridge.

MINE COUNTERMEASURES VESSELS

Minelayer

| Abdiel (N21) | 1967-1988 |

Was designated as a headquarters and support ship for Mine Counter-measures vessels and to lay exercise mines.

Ton Class

Alfriston (M1103)	1954-1986
Bickington (M1109)	1954-1986
Bildeston (M1110)	1953-1986
Brereton (M1113)	1954-1992
Brinton (M1114)	1954-1993
Bronington (M1115)	1954-1988
Wilton (M1116)	1973-1994
Crichton (M1124)	1954-1985
Cuxton (M1125)	1954-1991
Bossington (M1133)	1956-1987
Gavinton (M1140)	1954-1990
Glasserton (M1141)	1954-1980
Hodgeston (M1146)	1954-1986
Hubberston (M1147)	1955-1991
Iveston (M1151)	1955-1992
Kedleston (M1153)	1955-1991
Kellington (M1154)	1955-1992
Kirkliston (M1157)	1954-1990
Laleston (M1158)	1954-1981
Maxton (M1165)	1957-1988
Nurton (M1166)	1957-1993
Pollington (M1173)	1958-1985
Shavington (M1180)	1956-1985
Sheraton (M1181)	1956-1993
Upton (M1187)	1956-1991
Walkerton (M1188)	1958-1986
Wotton (M1195)	1957-1992
Soberton (M1200)	1957-1992
Stubbington (M1204)	1957-1986
Lewiston (M1208)	1960-1984
Crofton (M1216)	1958-1984

The RN operated over 30 Ton class MCMs during this period, comprising both minesweepers and minehunters. They were of wooden hull construction over an alloy frame (with the exception of Wilton, built in 1973 with a Glass Reinforced Plastic (GRP) hull - the largest vessel at that time to use this technique, and a prototype of the later Hunt and Sandown classes).

Hunt Class

Brecon (M29)	1980-2005
Ledbury (M30)	1981-Pres
Cattistock (M31)	1982-Pres
Cottesmore (M32)	1983-2005
Brocklesby (M33)	1983-Pres
Middleton (M34)	1984-Pres
Dulverton (M35)	1983-2005
Bicester (M36)	1986-2000
Chiddingfold (M37)	1984-Pres
Atherstone (M38)	1987-Pres
Hurworth (M39)	1985-Pres
Berkeley (M40)	1988-2001
Quorn (M41)	1989-Pres

Built of GRP, these vessels were designed for both minehunting and minesweeping, although the latter role has now been replaced by modern remote systems which seek out the mines and which are subsequently counter-mined by remote vehicles.

Sandown Class

Sandown	1989-2005

The first of a new class of 12 single role mine-hunters. They were built in two batches by Vosper Thornycroft, Woolston. Five Batch 1 vessels were commissioned between 1989 and 1993. Batch 2 design changes included accommodation for female officers and rat-ings, bigger Voith Schneider propulsion units, a more powerful crane for UAV deployment and an improved decompression chamber. The last of the class was delivered in 2001.

EDATS Type

St David (M07)	1972-1983
Venturer (M08)	1973-1983

These two vessels were commercial trawlers (Suffolk Monarch and Suffolk Harvester re-spectively) chartered by the Royal Navy to prove the Extra Deep Armed Team Sweep concept. There was at the time a perceived threat to ballistic missile armed submarines from mines laid deep off the continental shelf. These ships trialled the concept of sweeping with wires to a depth of 300m using explosive cutters rather than serrated sweep wires. Such was the weight of the sweep wire that

two vessels were required to tow the sweep. They were returned to their owners in 1983.

River Class

Waveney (M2003)	1984-1993
Carron (M2004)	1984-1993
Dovey (M2005)	1985-1993
Helford (M2006)	1985-1993
Humber (M2007)	1985-1994
Blackwater (M2008)	1985-1997
Itchen (M2009)	1986-1997
Helmsdale (M2010)	1986-1993
Orwell (M2011)	1986-2000
Ribble (M2012)	1986-1993
Spey (M2013)	1986-1997
Arun (M2014)	1986-1997

A class of Extra Deep Armed Team Sweep vessels designed to meet the threat of minelaying in deep waters. Most were oper-ated by the Royal Navy Reserve. In 1993 it was announced that the RNR vessels were to be paid off as part of the post Cold War peace dividend. In 1994 seven vessels were put up for disposal while Blackwater, Arun, Itchen and Spey were refitted as patrol vessels to op-erate in the Northern Ireland Squadron, their task, to deter the movement of arms, muni-tions and personnel of the various terrorist fac-tions that existed within the province. Orwell ended her days as a Navigational Training ship attached to the Britannia Royal Naval College. On decommissioning many were

transfered to Foreign navies for further serv-ice in a variety of roles.

Requisitioned Trawler Type

Pict	1973-1982
Junella	1975-1982
Farnella	1972-1982
Northella	1973-1998
Cordella	1973-1982

Five deep sea trawlers requisitioned by the MoD during the Falklands crisis and converted to EDATS minesweepers to clear the waters around the islands. They formed the 11th Mine Counter Measures Squadron and were manned predominantly by members of the 1st MCM Squadron. On completion of the minesweeping operation in July 1982 they re-turned to the UK and were returned to their owners. Northella was further charted for se-curity operations on the Clyde and as a Navi-gational Training vessel.

Ley Class

Aveley (M2002)	1954-1983
Isis (M2010)	1955-1982

Designed as Inshore Minehunters, the ships were latterly used as training ships, which to-gether with the Ham class below were re-placed by the Fleet Tender type training ships (see page 11).

Ham Class

Dittisham (M2621)	1954-1982
Flintham (M2628)	1955-1982
Thornham (M2793)	1958-1984

The survivors of a large class of Inshore Minesweepers built in the 1950s these ships were latterly used for initial sea training.

PATROL & TRAINING VESSELS

Island Class

Anglesey (P277)	1979-2003
Alderney (P278)	1979-2002
Orkney (P299)	1977-1999
Jersey (P295)	1976-1993
Guernsey (P297)	1977-2003
Shetland (P298)	1977-2002
Lindisfarne (P300)	1978-2003

The Island-class patrol vessel was first designed and built for the Scottish Fisheries Protection Agency. As a result of the RN's success with the loaned SFPA vessel Jura, the RN built a further seven. The vessels formed the Offshore Division, which, in addition to their fishery protection tasks outside the 12-mile coastal limit, carried out regular surveillance patrols of the offshore gas and oilfield installations. Most now operating with overseas navies.

Castle Class

Leeds Castle (P258)	1981-2005
Dumbarton Castle (P265)	1982-2008

Originally to have been a class of four offshore patrol vessels, the programme was stopped at just two. With the end of the Falklands War one of the class was on permanent deployment to the islands at any one time. They had a large flightdeck aft which could accommodate a Sea King sized helicopter.

Ton Class

Beachampton (P1007)	1954-1985
Monkton (P1055)	1957-1985
Wasperton (P1089)	1957-1984
Wolverton (P1093)	1958-1984
Yarnton (P1096)	1957-1984

Former Ton class MCM vessels which were converted for the patrol boat role in the waters surrounding Hong Kong. They had limited armour and a second 40/60 Bofors gun, in addition to extra machine gun positions.

Peacock Class

Peacock (P239)	1984-1997
Plover (P240)	1984-1997
Starling (P241)	1984-1997
Swallow (P242)	1984-1988
Swift (P243)	1984-1988

The five ships of this class were built by Hall Russell, Aberdeen to replace the elderly Ton class serving as the Hong Kong Patrol Squadron. They were 75% financed by the Colony and commissioned into RN service in 1983 and 1984 and operated as the 6th Patrol Craft Squadron. HMS Swallow and Swift were transferred to the Irish Naval Service in 1988.

Bird Class

Kingfisher (P260)	1975-1994
Cygnet (P261)	1976-1996
Peterel (P262)	1977-1990
Sandpiper (P263)	1977-1990
Cormorant (P256)	1976-1990
Hart (P257)	1972-1990
Redpole (P259)	1967-1996

Originally a class of four vessels based on the RAF Seal class long range recovery craft. They were initially employed on coastal patrol and fishery protection duties. They were augmented by Redpole (ex-Sea Otter) and Cormorant and Hart (two ex-RAF Spitfire class vessels (ex-Sunderland and Stirling). The latter two vessels were slightly smaller and operated in and around the waters of Gibraltar Bay. The remaining vessels were found to be poor seaboats and quite unsuitable for operations in the rougher areas of the North Sea. Two of the ships were transferred to anti-terror operations off Northern Ireland while the remainder were fitted with an enclosed upper bridge and employed as training ships attached to the Royal Naval College at Dartmouth.

Sword Class

Scimitar (P271)	1970-1981
Cutlass (P274)	1970-1981
Sabre (P275)	1970-1981

Developed from the very successful Brave Class, these three vessels were operated by the Fast Training Boat Squadron. Unarmed, they were used in the training role to give the Fleet more experience of the capabilities of fast, modern attack craft, then becoming available to potential enemies.

Tenacity Class

Tenacity (P276)	1970-1985

A private venture boat built by Vosper Thornycroft, Portsmouth in 1969. She was purchased by the RN in January 1972 and underwent conversion by Vosper Thornycroft, to operate in the Fisheries Protection role.

Attacker Class

Attacker (P281)	1983-1991
Chaser (P282)	1983-1992
Fencer (P283)	1983-1992
Hunter (P284)	1983-1991

Striker (P285)	1983-1991

Built by Fairey Allday, these five vessels were operated as patrol and training craft. HMS Attacker, Hunter and Striker formed the Cyprus Squadron and were used for patrol and harbour protection. The remainder were allocated to University units. All were withdrawn from service in the early 1990s and transferred to the Lebanese Navy.

P2000 Class

Express (P163)	1988-Pres
Explorer (P164)	1985-Pres
Example (P165)	1985-Pres
Exploit (P167)	1988-Pres
Archer (P264)	1985-Pres
Biter (P270)	1986-Pres
Smiter (P272)	1986-Pres
Pursuer (P273)	1988-Pres
Blazer (P279)	1988-Pres
Dasher (P280)	1988-Pres
Puncher (P291)	1988-Pres
Charger (P292)	1988-Pres
Ranger (P293)	1988-Pres
Trumpeter (P294)	1988-Pres

Fourteen Fast Training Boats that made up the Inshore Training Squadron Ranger and Trumpeter served with the Gibraltar Patrol Boat Squadron. Pursuer and Dasher were deployed to Cyprus in a similar role in 2002. All now form part of the 1st Patrol Boat Squadron and sup-

port the various University Royal Navy Units. Two are employed on security operations on the Clyde. Four vessels (names beginning "Ex") were originally acquired for the RNXS before being transfered to the RN.

Falkland Islands Patrol Vessels

Protector (P244)	1983-1986
Guardian (P245)	1983-1986
Sentinel (P246)	1984-1992

Former ice-strengthened oilrig support vessels acquired in 1983 and converted for Falkland Island patrol duties. Commercial names were Seaforth Champion, Seaforth Saga and Seaforth Warrior respectively. Following a refit in 1987 Sentinel went on to replace Wakeful as Clyde patrol ship and a support vessel to submarines working up in the Clyde area.

Ford Class

Dee (P3104)	1953-1983
Droxford (P3113)	1954-1986

Former Seaward Defence Boats, these remaining two vessels were used as University unit training boats attached to Liverpool and Glasgow universities respectively.

Loyal Class

Alert (P252)	1974-1985

Vigilant (P254)	1974-1986
Loyal Watcher (A159)	1978-1997
Loyal Chancellor (A1770)	1978-1997

Members of the Loyal class training vessels used by the RNXS (Alert ex-Loyal Governor; Vigilant ex-Loyal Factor), these two vessels were employed by the Royal Navy for counter-terrorism operations in Northern Irish waters. On completion of RN operations they were re-named Lydford and Meavy respectively. Loyal Chancellor and Loyal Watcher were operated by the University Royal Navy Unit before being replaced by the newer P2000 class.

Fleet Tender Type

Manly (A92)	1982-1991
Mentor (A94)	1982-1991
Milbrook (A97)	1982-1991
Messina (A107)	1982-1991

Similar to the Loyal class training vessels, they were operated by the RN for initial sea training for new entry trainees. They had inside stairs down and watertight doors going forward, with the two holds divided into five bunkrooms.

Hovercraft

SRN 6 (XV615) (P236)	1967-1982
SRN 6 (XV617) (P237)	1967-1982
SRN 6 (XV852) (P238)	1967-1984
BH 7 (XW255) (P235)	1969-1985

VT 2 (P234)	1979-1982

The three types of hovercraft were operated by the Naval Hovercraft Trials Unit (formerly the Interservice Hovercraft Trials Unit). All were fully amphibious and used on fleet exercises and in a variety of trials ranging from logistics support to mine countermeasures. They were based at HMS Daedalus at Lee-on-Solent. Two SRN-6 hovercraft were deployed to Hong Kong on anti-immigrant patrols.

Hydrofoil

Speedy (P296)	1980-1982

A Boeing Jetfoil, she was procured in 1979 to provide the RN with practical experience in the operation of a hydrofoil, to ascertain technical and performance characteristics, and to oversee the capability of such a craft in the Fishery Protection Squadron.

SURVEY VESSELS

Ocean Survey

Hecla (A133)	1965-1997
Hecate (A137)	1965-1991
Herald (A138)	1974-2001
Hydra (A144)	1966-1986

The Hecla class formed the backbone of the Royal Navy's ocean survey fleet during this period. Hecla, Hecate and Hydra, were ordered in the early 1960s while Herald was ordered in the 1970s. All, bar Hecate, saw Service in the Falklands war as ambulance ships. Both Herald and Hecate served as a patrol vessel in the Falklands area post war, during which time they were armed with 20mm Oerlikons and painted grey.

Coastal Survey

Bulldog (A317)	1968-2001
Beagle (A319)	1968-2002
Fox (A320)	1968-1989
Fawn (A335)	1968-1991

Designed as coastal survey vessels, these four vessels were originally intended to work overseas in pairs, but latterly were employed mainly in home waters.

Roebuck (A130)	1986-2010

An enlarged and improved variant of the Bulldog class she was intended to operate around the UK continental shelf but, as the survey fleet shrank, she found herself regularly deploying overseas.

Inshore Survey

Echo (A70)	1958-1984
Enterprise (A71)	1959-1984
Egeria (A72)	1959-1984

Based on the hull of the Ham class, these three vessels were designed to operate in shallow waters such as harbour approaches, shipping lanes, rivers and estuaries. Together, the ships of this class formed the RN's Inshore Survey Squadron.

Waterwitch (M2720)	1960-1985
Woodlark (M2780)	1959-1985

The former Ham class minesweepers Powderham and Yaxham, they were converted to augment the Echo class.

Survey Launch

Gleaner (A86)	1983-Pres

Carrying the prefix HMSML (Her Majesty's Survey Motor Launch) Gleaner was designed to conduct inshore surveys along the south coast of England, though she has since surveyed all around the coastline of Great Britain.

Ice Patrol Ship

Endurance (A171)	1968-1991

The former Danish merchant vessel, Anita Dan, built in 1956 by Grogerwerft for the Lauritzen Lines, she was acquired by the RN in 1967 and converted by Harland & Wolff for operations as an Ice Patrol ship in Antarctica.

OCEAN-GOING TUG

Wakeful (A236)	1965-1988

She was built in 1965 and commissioned into the RN in 1974 for fishery protection duties. From 1976 she operated on the Clyde as a submarine support vessel.

SEABED OPERATIONS VESSEL

Challenger (K07)	1984-1990

A purpose-built state of the art vessel to support deep sea operations and saturation diving. She was fitted with a dynamic positioning system, allowing her to remain stationary over her target. She could recover divers and their diving bell through a moonpool in the hull and had a gantry aft for deploying submersibles. She also had a flightdeck to accommodate a helicopter. Due to defence cuts, the ship was seen as a luxury and decommissioned in 1990.

ROYAL YACHT

Britannia (A00)	1954-1997

Designed as a medium-sized naval hospital ship for 200 patients, the vessel was used as a Royal Yacht in peacetime.

ROYAL FLEET AUXILIARY

FAST FLEET TANKERS

Improved Tide Class

Tidepool (A75)	1963-1982
Tidespring (A76)	1963-1991

A development of the earlier Tide class, these Fleet tankers were equipped with a single spot flightdeck and a hangar to operate helicopters.

Ol Class

Olwen (A122)	1965-2000
Olna (A123)	1966-2000
Olmeda (A124)	1965-1994

Fast fleet tankers tasked with providing fuel, food, ammunition and other supplies to RN vessels around the world. The three ships in the class were an evolution of the earlier Tide class.

SMALL FLEET TANKERS

Rover Class

Green Rover (A268)	1969-1988
Grey Rover (A269)	1970-2006
Blue Rover (A270)	1970-1993
Gold Rover (A271)	1974-Pres
Black Rover (A273)	1974-Pres

A class of small fleet tanker tasked to support RN warships. Can refuel abeam or astern and have a helicopter platform aft for vertical replenishment.

SUPPORT TANKERS

Leaf Class

Pearleaf (A77)	1960-1986
Plumleaf (A78)	1960-1986

The remaining pair of eight similar tankers bare-boat chartered for freighting duties. They were subsequently fitted with a single RAS station to allow abeam refuelling.

Appleleaf (A79)	1979-1989
Bayleaf (A109)	1982-2011
Brambleleaf (A81)	1979-2007
Orangeleaf (A110)	1989-1900

These four vessels originally formed part of a 4-ship order for commercial owners who subsequently ran into financial difficulties and were unable to accept the ships. The MoD chartered the ships and they were fitted with increased accommodation space and RAS facilities for refuelling both abeam and astern. Appleleaf was transferred to Australia and renamed HMAS Westralia.

Oakleaf (A111)	1986-2007

A larger vessel than the previous four leaf class she was bareboat chartered by the MoD, entering service in 1986. She had similar RAS capabilities to the earlier vessels. All of the Leaf class vessels were capable of conducting pump-over operations allowing them to transfer their oil cargo to another tanker.

COASTAL TANKERS

Eddy Class

Eddyfirth (A261)	1954-1981

The sole survivor of a class of eight such coastal tankers. Originally intended to be Attendant tankers, this role was overtaken by advances in replenishment at sea methods, so she spent most of her time transfering fuels and liquids between base ports.

STORE SHIPS

Ness Class

Stromness (A344)	1967-1983
Tarbatness (A345)	1967-1980

Two remaining vessels from an original class of three. Designed as Stores Support ships they carried thousands of items of Naval, Victualling Armament and Air Stores which could be transferred by jackstay or helicopter. Following RFA service all three went on to see extensive careers with the US Military Sealift Command.

Fort Class

Fort Austin (A386)	1979-Pres
Fort Grange (A385)	1978-Pres

A further development of the Ness class this pair of ships were equipped with extensive flightdeck and hangar facilities enabling them to embark and operate helicopters in an operational role.

ARMAMENTS STORES SHIPS

Regent Class

Regent (A486)	1967-1992
Resource (A480)	1967-1997

RFA munitions replenishment ships certified to store and supply the fleet with munitions, including nuclear weapons. They became the first RFA's to be allocated permanent Flights (and carried Wessex HU5 helicopters from 829 NAS until April 1987) as they were fitted with full aviation facilities.

STORES CARRIER

Bacchus Class

Bacchus (A404)	1962-1981

Operated by the RFA on long-term bareboat charter, the ship was used to move stores from base to base, worldwide.

LOGISTIC LANDING SHIPS

Sir Class

Sir Bedivere (L3004)	1967-2008
Sir Galahad (L3005)	1966-1982
Sir Geraint (L3027)	1967-2003
Sir Lancelot (L3029)	1964-1989
Sir Percivale (L3036)	1968-2004
Sir Tristram (L3505)	1967-2005

A class Landing Ship Logistics (LSL), designed for amphibious warfare missions, in support of the major amphibious ships. They had both bow and stern doors leading onto the main vehicle deck, making them roll-on/roll-off, combined with ramps that lead to upper and lower vehicle decks. Their shallow draft enabled them to beach themselves and use the bow doors for speedy unloading of troops and equipment. Sir Galahad and Sir Tristram were badly damaged during the Falklands War, with Sir Galahad being towed out to sea and sunk.

Sir Caradoc (L3522)	1983-1988
Sir Lamorak (L3532)	1983-1986

Two commercial Ro-Ro vessels chartered after the Falklands war to provide cover while Sir Tristram was repaired and the new Sir Galahad completed.

Sir Galahad (II) (L3005)	1987-2007

Ordered as a replacement for the vessel sunk in 1982, she carried the same name and pennant number as her predecessor. Unlike the previous vessel which had traditional landing craft doors in the bow, she was fitted with a visor type bow door, that opened upwards.

FORWARD REPAIR SHIP

Diligence (A132)	1984-Pres

As MV Stena Inspector, the ship was taken up from trade during the Falklands War where she repaired many damaged RN & RFA vessels. She was purchased by the MoD in 1983 and renamed Diligence.

DIVING VESSEL

Seaforth Clansman	1978-1987

Taken over by the RFA on charter to cover whilst Challenger was building. She was based at Aberdeen with NP1007 embarked.

AVIATION SUPPORT SHIPS

Engadine (K08)	1967-1989

A helicopter Support ship used for flying training. Her flight deck was extended in 1984 to allow for operation of the Sea King helicopter.

Argus (A135)	1988-Pres

As the container vessel MV Contender Bezant, she was taken up from trade during the Falklands War. She was purchased in 1984 and converted to support helicopter flying training. Much larger and more capable than Engadine she also had a secondary role as a Primary Casualty Receiving Ship.

Reliant (A131)	1983-1986

Another vessel taken up from trade during the Falklands War. Originally named MV Astronomer, she was converted to test the US Navy Arapaho containerised concept for aviation support, equipping the ship with a prefabricated flight deck and hangars formed from containers. The trials were not deemed successful and the ship was sold in 1986.

HMS ABDIEL

Built by Vosper Thornycroft as an exercise minelayer, ABDIEL was completed in 1967. In 1974 she acted as command ship for the mine clearance operations in the Suez Canal. In addition to her workshop facilities she could accommodate a full headquarters support staff when required. She operated in the Persian Gulf supporting MCM vessels before finally paying off in 1988. She was sold and towed to Spain for breaking up in September that year.

(Syd Goodman Collection)

HMS ACTIVE

Built by Vosper Thornycroft and completed in 1977 she was one of five of the class to be fitted with the Exocet missile from build (seen here in front of the bridge). In 1978 she was involved in oil clean up operations in the North Sea after the Greek tanker ELENE V was cut in half by another vessel. In 1982 she took part in the Falklands War conducting NGS operations against shore targets during the final assault on Port Stanley. Prolonged operations in heavy seas and increased weight took its toll on the hull and all of the class received strengthening patches along the hull in later life. She was decommissioned in 1994 and transferred to Pakistan and renamed SHAH JAHAN.

(Crown Copyright/MoD 1986)

HMS AJAX

Built by Cammell Laird, Birkenhead, she was originally laid down as the Type 12 frigate FOWEY, but completed as a Leander class frigate in 1964. She initially served with the 24 EG in the Far East and in 1970 operated as the Gibraltar guardship. In 1970 she entered refit at Devonport, emerging in 1973 as an Ikara conversion, her twin 4.5-inch turret being replaced by an Ikara ASW missile launcher. During the conversion the two 40mm were repositioned from the hangar roof to aft of the bridge wings and two quad Seacat launchers mounted in their place. She paid off in 1985, becoming a harbour training ship at Devonport. In 1988 she arrived at Millom, Cumbria, for breaking up. *(Crown Copyright/MoD)*

HMS ALACRITY

Built by Yarrow and completed in 1977, in time to participate in the Silver Jubilee Fleet Review at Spithead, held in June that year. In 1980 she deployed to the Far East and was one of a group of RN ships to sail up the Yangtse river, the first to do so since AMETHYST. She participated in the Falklands War, and during a night transit of Falkland Sound (to determine whether it was mined) she encountered and sank the Argentine transport vessel ISLA DE LOS ESTADOS. She spent time in the Gulf prior to refitting and receiving hull strengthening in 1983. In 1989 she was on station in the Caribbean and provided support in the wake of hurricane Hugo. She decommissioned in 1994, transferring to Pakistan as BADR.   *(Crown Copyright/MoD 1983)*

HMS AMAZON

She was the lead ship of the Type 21 class, being built by Vosper Thornycroft and completing in 1974. Initial armament comprised a single Mk8 4.5-inch gun, a quadruple Seacat launcher on the hangar roof and two 20mm Oerlikons aft of the bridge wings. She was later fitted with Exocet ahead of the bridge. Initially operated with a Wasp helicopter, but following trials in 1978 all of the class were cleared to operate the more capable Lynx. Her ASW capability was increased later with the installation of two triple torpedo tubes. She was the only Type 21 not to sail for the South Atlantic in 1982 as she was deployed to the Gulf. She decommissioned in 1993, becoming BABUR in Pakistani Navy service.

(Crown Copyright/MoD)

HMS AMBUSCADE

Built by Yarrow and completed in 1975. In 1977 she operated with the SNFL and in 1979, while at Devonport, was damaged when a dockside crane toppled across the ship in extreme weather. In late 1981 she was in the Persian Gulf, and in 1982 deployed to the South Atlantic for operations off the Falklands. Following a collision with USS DALE, in the Indian Ocean in 1983, she had to have a new bow section fitted (constructed by Mazagon Docks) at Bombay. As with the rest of the class she suffered hull cracking and underwent a restorative refit and hull strengthening. She decommissioned in 1993 and was transfered to the Pakistan Navy where she served as PNS TARIQ.   *(Crown Copyright/MoD)*

HMS ANTELOPE

The second of the Type 21 class, she was built by Vosper Thornycroft and completed in 1975. In 1981, during a patrol off Belize, she seized £30 million of marijuana from a merchant vessel. She sailed with the Falklands Task Force in 1982. On 23 May, while in San Carlos Water, she came under attack from Argentine Skyhawk aircraft ans suffered two direct hits from 1000lb bombs, though both failed to explode. She was moved to more sheltered waters where attempts were made to make the bombs safe, however, one detonated, killing one member of the EOD team, and the ship was abandoned as magazines exploded throughout the night. With her back broken, she sank at anchor the following morning. *(Crown Copyright/MoD)*

HMS ANTRIM

Built by Fairfields and completed in 1970 she was one of four Batch 2 County class destroyers, recognised by the larger double bedstead Type 965 radar on the mainmast. In the mid-1970s four Exocet missiles were fitted in place of 'B' turret. She led the force that recaptured South Georgia in 1982, her Wessex helicopter being responsible for the rescue of 16 SAS soldiers from Fortuna Glacier after their helicopters were destroyed in white-out conditions during the operation. She was hit by a bomb in San Carlos Water that failed to explode. She decommissioned in 1984 and was sold to Chile where she was renamed ALMIRANTE COCHRANE and converted to a helicopter carrier.

(Crown Copyright/MoD)

HMS APOLLO

A Broad-beamed Leander, built by Yarrow and completed in 1972, she was one of a handful of the class to retain her 4.5-inch gun throughout her RN career. In 1973 she took part in the second Cod War off Iceland, being rammed by the ICGV AEGIR on 29 August. The 1981 defence cuts, meant that the ship would not receive her intended modernisation and in 1982 she was deployed to the South Atlantic to patrol the Falkland Island waters after the war. She is seen here returning to Devonport on completion of the patrol with pennant numbers painted out and additional 20mm on the quarterdeck. She decommissioned in 1988 and was transferred to Pakistan, serving as ZULFIQUAR until 2006. *(Crown Copyright/MoD)*

HMS ARDENT

Built by Yarrow she was completed in 1977. In 1978 she deployed to the Baltic and between 1979-81 spent much time East of Suez. In 1982 she formed part of the Falklands Task Force. On 21 May, whilst operating in Falkland Sound bombarding the Argentine airstrip at Goose Green, she was attacked by at least three waves of Argentine aircraft. In the initial attack two bombs exploded in the hangar and a third penetrated the hull but failed to detonate. Within 20 minutes a further five aircraft attacked hitting the ship aft and causing fatal damage. Fires were out of control and the ship was abandoned, finally sinking the following day. 22 of her crew were killed.   *(Crown Copyright/MoD)*

HMS ARETHUSA

Built by J.S. White at Cowes and completed in 1965, she was one of the first to receive the Seacat missile system from build. She took part in the Second Cod War, colliding with the ICGV ODINN on 10 August 1973. She emerged from an Ikara conversion in 1977. She is seen here with SCOT radomes on the foremast. These were fitted as required for operations. In 1985 she was fitted with towed array sonar (removed from LOWESTOFT), mounted centrally on the quarterdeck. The VDS well was plated in and the Limbo removed and the well plated over to accommodate the sound room. The ship was decommissioned in 1985 and sunk as a target in 1991.

(Crown Copyright/MoD)

HMS ARGONAUT

ARGONAUT was built by Hawthorn Leslie and completed in 1967. She was modernised at Devonport between 1976-80 with four Exocet containers in lieu of the 4.5-inch gun and three quadruple Seacat missile launchers (one forward of the Exocet and two on the hangar roof). The Limbo was removed and the well plated over to allow operation of the larger Lynx helicopter. She was badly damaged during the Falklands War, being hit by two 1000lb bombs. Towed array was fitted to the quarterdeck in 1983 and she paid off in 1993, being broken up in Spain from 1995.

(Crown Copyright/MoD)

RFA ARGUS

Built by Cantieri Navale Breda SpA, Venice, as the containership CONTENDER BEZANT, she was requisitioned during the Falklands War in 1982. In 1984 she was converted at Harland & Wolff, Belfast, to operate as an Aviation Training Ship to replace ENGADINE. She was formally renamed in 1987. She had a secondary role as a Primary Casualty Receiving Ship, with a 100 bed hospital. Following an extensive update in 2007 this is now her primary role and she has deployed to both war zones and on humanitarian operations as such. *(Crown Copyright/MoD)*

HMS ARIADNE

Built by Yarrow and completed in 1972 ARIADNE was the last of the Leander class to be completed. She retained her 4.5-inch turret throughout her career. In 1973 she deployed to the waters off Iceland to conduct Cod War patrols and in 1986 assisted with flood relief operations in Jamaica. In 1991 she served in the Dartmouth Training Squadron, ending her RN career in 1992. She was sold to Chile where she served until 1998 as the GENERAL BAQUEDANO. She was sunk as a target in 2004.

(Crown Copyright/MoD)

HMS ARK ROYAL

She was built by Swan Hunter and completed in 1985, the last of the Invincible class. Designed primarily as an ASW ship she could carry a mix of 22 aircraft - Sea King helicopters for ASW and AEW and Sea Harriers for air defence. She led a deployment to Australia in 1988 and to the US east coast in 1990. Her aircraft conducted combat patrols over the former Yugoslavia. She was in reserve from 1994 until completing refit in 2001, emerging without Sea Dart and with an extended flightdeck. She was part of the task group deployed to the Gulf during the Iraq War in 2003. In 2011 she decommissioned, together with all UK Harrier aircraft, a victim to the 2010 SDSR. *(Crown Copyright/MoD)*

HMS ARROW

Built by Yarrow and commissioned in 1976 at Sunderland, her affiliated town. She was the first to complete with Exocet missiles. She deployed to the Far East in 1979 and in 1981 served with SNFL. She deployed with the Falklands Task Force in 1982, where she became the first RN vessel damaged (being strafed by cannon fire) and the first to engage the enemy (firing on land forces a Port Stanley). She came to the rescue of SHEFFIELD, when hit, fighting fires and evacuating 225 of her crew. She also helped the firefighting effort after PLYMOUTH was attacked. She underwent refit at Devonport in 1983 returning to the South Atlantic in 1984. She was transfered to Pakistan as KHAIBAR in 1994.   *(Crown Copyright/MoD 1989)*

HMS ATHERSTONE

Built by Vosper Thornycroft and completed in 1986, she is one of thirteen Hunt class MCMVs built for the RN. Originally, they combined the separate role of the traditional minesweeper and that of the active minehunter in one hull, however, the traditional wire sweep method was decommissioned in 2005 and mine disposal is now carried out by unmanned submersible craft deployed by the parent vessel and able to detect, classify and destroy mines. ATHERSTONE returned to Portsmouth in 2010 after 2 years forward deployed to the Persian Gulf. These long deployments are made possible by crew changes abroad - in this instance five such changes took place. *(Crown Copyright/MoD)*

HMS AURORA

Built by John Brown and completed in 1964, she was assigned to 2 TS at Portland as leader. Deployed in 1972 on Cod War duties, she went to the aid of a blazing Icelandic fishing vessel, rescuing five crewmen. She underwent Ikara conversion at Chatham from 1973-76. The original cost of a Leander class frigate was just shy of £5 million - a similar amount was esti-mated for the Ikara conversion but in reality cost anything from £7million - £23 million. She decommissioned in 1987 and was sold to DML at Devonport who intended to upgrade her and sell her on. This plan fell through and she was scrapped at Millom in 1990.

(Crown Copyright/MoD 1986)

HMS AVELEY

An Inshore Minehunter, she was built by J. Samuel Whites and completed in 1954. Similar to the Ham class, but with less power as they were not required to tow sweeps, AVELEY initially served with the 51st MS at Port Edgar prior to entering reserve at Rosneath in 1957. She returned to service in 1963 operating as a training tender at Devonport, a role she retained until she finally paid off in 1982. *(Crown Copyright/MoD 1979)*

HMS AVENGER

The eight and final Type 21 frigate, she was built by Yarrow and completed in 1978. She operated in the West Indies, North Atlantic, Mediterranean and Gulf of Oman prior to the Falkands War. In May 1982 she deployed to the Falklands as part of the Bristol reinforcement group, arriving in time to assist in the final bombardment of Port Stanley. She returned to the UK in September. In 1988 she received a trial installation of a hydraulically actuated trim flap on her stern (see photo) in an effort to improve efficiency and economical operation of the engines. She was decommissioned and sold to Pakistan in 1994 where she served as TIPPU SULTAN. *(Crown Copyright/MoD)*

HMS BATTLEAXE

Built by Yarrow and completed in 1980 she was the second of the Batch I Type 22 frigates to enter service. Designed as a specialist ASW ship, she was equipped with a hangar to support two Lynx helicopters as her primary ASW weapon. She was also equipped with two triple STWS. Her main armament was four Exocet missiles for anti-ship warfare and two sextuple Seawolf launchers (one forward and one aft) for AA and anti-missile warfare. She was one of only two completed with a large funnel with widely spaced exhausts - this was later changed for the more streamlined funnel fitted to the rest of the class. She was decommissioned in 1997 and transfered to Brazil as RADEMAKER. *(Crown Copyright/MoD)*

RFA BAYLEAF

Completed in 1982 by Cammell Laird, she was originally to be a commercial vessel named HUDSON SOUND. A STaT 32 Product Tanker she was bareboat chartered by the MoD for service with the RFA. Almost immediately she was deployed to support the Falklands campaign, sailing in company with INTREPID and replenishing the liner QE2, which had been requisitioned for use as a troopship. Together with BRAMBLELEAF and ORGANGELEAF she spent extended periods operating east of Suez - her final deployment being for 18 months in the Gulf. She decommissioned in 2011.

(Crown/Copyright/MoD 1986)

HMS BEACHAMPTON

Built by Goolie Shipbuilding Co Ltd, she was completed in 1954 and served with the 5th MSS at Portsmouth from 1958-64. Following a refit at Portsmouth in 1965 she went on to serve with the 9th MSS in the Persian Gulf. In 1971 she sailed for Hong Kong, with her sister YARNTON, where she was refitted and redesignated as a Patrol Craft for operation with the 6th Hong Kong Patrol Squadron. Her pennant number was changed from M1107 to P1007 and she was fitted with a second 40mm Bofors gun aft of the funnel. She paid off in 1985 and was broken up at Hong Kong.

(Crown Copyright/MoD)

HMS BEAGLE

Built by Brooke Marine, Lowestoft, she was completed in 1968. Built to commercial standards for a reported cost of £53 million, these ships were designed to operate in pairs conducting coastal and shallow water surveys around the world. In the event they spent much time in UK waters surveying waters around UK offshore facilities. In a military role could support amphibious operations by conducting route surveys into landing sites. In 1998 this increased operational role was reflected in the ships being painted grey and displaying a pennant number. She decommissioned in 2002 and was sold for conversion to a luxury yacht, operating as MV TITAN with accommodation for 22 guests and a crew of 20. *(Crown Copyright/MoD)*

HMS BEAVER
Built by Yarrow and completed in 1984 she is an example of a Batch II Type 22, or a 'Stretched 22'. They had a heavily raked bow and were 55ft longer than the Batch I frigates, the "stretch" being between the foremast and the bridge. The weapon fit was the same as the earlier ships with four Exocet forward and two sextuple Seawolf launchers (one forward and one aft) She retained the small flight deck and hangar of the earlier ships, being able to operate two Lynx helicopters. The Type 22s carried emblems on their superstructure unique to each ship. She was decommissioned in 1999 and scrapped in Turkey in 2001.

(Crown Copyright/MoD)

BH7

The BH7 (or Wellington Class) was a 55 ton hovercraft designed and built by the British Hovercraft Corporation specifically for naval and military roles. The sole prototype, designated BH7 Mk2 was operated by the RN from 1970 being evaluated in a variety of different roles including fishery protection, ASW and MCM work. She was fitted with operational mine hunting equipment comprising Plessey 193M and 2048 Speedscan sonar. The concept was not adopted by the RN but later variants saw service in small numbers with the Iranian Navy. *(Crown Copyright/MoD)*

HMS BIRMINGHAM

The second Type 42 destroyer to be completed was built by Cammell Laird and commissioned in 1976. She is seen here in her original configuration with the double bedstead Type 965 radar (later replaced by the modern Type 1022). Note the colourful Cheverton boat amidships, replaced post-Falklands War by a Vulcan Phalanx CIWS either side of the funnel. Though not involved in the Falklands campaign, she operated in the area in 1984 and also served with the Standing Naval Force Mediterranean as well as operations in the Gulf and Adriatic. She was the first of the Type 42s to decommission, paying off in 1999 and being towed to Spain for breaking up in 2000. *(Crown Copyright/MoD)*

RFA BLACK ROVER

One of five Rover class small fleet tankers intended to replace the earlier Ranger class. She was built by Swan Hunter and completed in 1974. Together with GOLD ROVER, she had improved accommodation and different stern anchor arrangements to the earlier three ships. This design has proved very successful and the Rover class have supported ships in most operational theatres. BLACK ROVER spent much time in the Caribbean supporting ships on humanitarian and counter-drugs operations. She remains (2012) in service - at only 38 years-old!   *(Crown Copyright/MoD)*

HMS BOXER

Built by Yarrow and completed in 1983 she was the first of the Batch II frigates, similar in all respects to BEAVER. These ships received very little in the way of armament change throughout their short life, other than an enhancement in their small calibre weapons brought about by lessons learned following the Falklands War. Her original two single 40mm Bofors, were replaced by two twin Gambo 30mm mountings. A further two single 30mm BMarc cannon were sited at maindeck level just aft of the forward superstructure. She decommissioned in 1999 and was sunk as a target in 2004. *(Crown Copyright/MoD 1988)*

HMS BRAVE

Built by Yarrow and completed in 1986, she was the first of the second group of Batch II Type 22s. She introduced the taller hangar and larger flightdeck to enable operation of the Sea King helicopter. She was the first to introduce the Type 911 tracker and introduced the CACS 4 Command and Control system. She was also the only Type 22 to have Spey gas turbines in lieu of the older Olympus and spent much time cruising at higher speeds than her sisters. She became fully operational in 1987, serving in the Falklands, Adriatic, the first Gulf War and Caribbean. She paid off in 1999 and was sunk as a target in 2004 by weapons fired by the submarine SCEPTRE and frigate ARGYLL.   *(Crown Copyright/MoD)*

HMS BRAZEN

Built by Yarrow and completed in 1982, four months ahead of schedule due to the Falklands War. She was part of the UK Task Group deployed to the Gulf during the first Gulf War and her helicopters (nicknamed *Brazen Hussy* and *Brazen Harlot*) were involved in attacking Iraqi fast patrol craft. She ran aground off Chile in 1995, being refloated by tugs the following day. She was transferred to Brazil in 1996 where she still serves (2012) as BOSSISIO.

(Crown Copyright/MoD)

HMS BRECON

Built by Vosper Thornycroft and completed in 1979, she was the lead ship of the GRP hulled Hunt class. She was deployed to the Falklands after the war and to the Persian Gulf in 1991 during the first Gulf War, for which she was fitted with additional 20mm cannon and satellite communications. In 1994 she became the first RN warship to be commanded by a female. In 1998 she was converted for operations with the Northern Ireland Squadron, having all her minesweeping gear removed and two RIBs and their handling cranes installed on the former sweep deck. She decommissioned in 2005 and in 2008 became a Static Training Ship on the River Tamar for new entry sailors at nearby HMS RALEIGH.   *(Crown Copyright/MoD)*

HMS BRERETON

She was completed in 1954, a product of Richards Ironworks at Lowestoft. She was attached to the South Wales Division RNVR, being renamed ST DAVID. She reverted to her original name in 1961 prior to refitting at Devonport and spending 3 years in reserve at Hythe. A period of operations with the FPS followed in 1965 with a minehunter conversion starting in 1966. She subsequently served with the 9th MSS at Bahrain (1968-71), FPS (1972-79), the Tyne and Mersey Divisions RNR (1979 & 1981). Following service with 3rd MCMS from 1986 she was paid off in 1991.

(Crown Copyright/MoD)

HMS BRILLIANT

Built by Yarrow and completed in 1981, the first of the Type 22 frigates to sport the smaller streamlined funnel. She was part of the Task Force that took part in the Falklands War. During that war she became the first RN warship to fire the Seawolf missile in combat when, on 12 May, she shot down three A-4 Skyhawks. In October 1990 she was the first vessel to embark WRNS as part of the Ships Company following the decision to allow women to serve at sea. In 1991 she was part of the Task Group deployed to the Gulf during the first Gulf War. She was the subject of a 'fly on the wall' TV documentary series in the early 1990s. She paid off in 1996 and was sold to Brazil and renamed DODSWORTH.   *(Crown Copyright/MoD)*

HMS BRISTOL

Ordered in 1963, she was the only survivor of a planned class of Type 82 escorts for the cancelled CVA-01 aircraft carrier project. Built by Swan Hunter she was completed in 1972. She spent many years trialling and working up experience with a raft of new systems including the Sea Dart and Ikara missile systems and the ADAWS-2 command system. She suffered a boiler room fire in 1974 but continued in service running with just her gas turbines, until refitted in 1976. She became an operational ship in 1979 and led the reinforcement Task Group to the Falklands in 1982. Being large and expensive to operate she was decommissioned in 1991 and today (2012) is a Harbour Training Ship at Portsmouth.   *(Crown Copyright/MoD)*

HMY BRITANNIA

The Royal Yacht was built by John Brown & Co. Ltd, Clydebank. She was launched by Her Majesty Queen Elizabeth II on 16 April 1953 and commissioned on 11 January 1954. During her career she conducted 696 foreign visits and 272 visits in British waters. In 1986 she evacuated over 1,000 refugees from the civil war in Aden. In theory she had a secondary role as a hospital ship, though this was never utilised. It has been reported that her real wartime role was that of a nuclear-refuge in the event of nuclear war, the ship sailing the lochs of Scotland, with key Royal and government members onboard. She decommissioned in 1997 and is now a museum ship on display at Leith, Scotland.   *(Crown Copyright/MoD)*

HMS BROADSWORD

The first of the 16 ship Type 22 class, she was built by Yarrows and completed in 1979. These were the first RN frigates designed from the outset with a missile only armament and the first to be designed using metric measurements. She took part in the 1982 Falklands War. On 25 May 1982 she was providing air defence support to COVENTRY. During an air attack her Seawolf system lost track and then reset allowing the attackers to get through. BROADSWORD was hit by one bomb, which bounced up through the flight deck and destroyed her Lynx helicopter. COVENTRY was sunk and the frigate rescued 170 of her crew. She decommissioned in 1995 and was transfered to Brazil as GREENHALGH.   *(Crown Copyright/MoD)*

HMS BRONINGTON

Built by Cook, Welton & Gemmell Ltd, Beverley, she was completed in 1954 serving initially with 101st RNVR Squadron being renamed HUMBER. She reverted to her original name in 1958 prior to entering refit at Chatham. In the 1960s she served with 50th MSS at Portland and 51st MSS at Port Edgar. She was perhaps most well-known for being the command of Lt HRH The Prince of Wales from 1976. She paid off in 1988 and was preserved for public display, first in Manchester and latterly at Birkenhead. She is now (2012) closed to the public and is in a poor state of repair. *(Crown Copyright/MoD)*

HMS BULLDOG

Sister ship to BEAGLE (see page 46) she was completed by Brooke Marine, Lowestoft, in 1968. Their elegant lines betray the yacht building pedigree of her builders. These elegant vessels were diesel-powered and had a reputation for being good sea boats. Their 'A' prefix to pennant numbers was changed to 'H' to reflect their naval rather than auxiliary role. She was decommissioned in 2001 and like BEAGLE was sold to new owners in New Zealand for conversion to a yacht. However, in 2004, while under conversion, she was seriously damaged by fire and all work was suspended.

(Crown Copyright/MoD 1990)

HMS CARDIFF

She was laid down and launched by Vickers at Barrow, but work on her was suspended, ironically, to allow Vickers to concentrate on the Type 42 HERCULES, being built for Argentina. CARDIFF was completed by Swan Hunters in 1979. It was because of the presence of Type 42s in the Argentine fleet, that during the Falklands War, RN Type 42s had a broad black band painted from the top of the funnel to the waterline as an identification mark. During the Gulf War in 1991 her Lynx helicopters destroyed two Iraqi minesweepers. She decommissioned in 2005. *(Crown Copyright/MoD)*

HMS CHALLENGER

She was built by Scotts at Greenock and entered service in 1984. A very expensive and specialist ship she could conduct saturation diving to great depths. A moonpool amidships allowed the deployment of a diving bell from which divers could transfer to a decompression chamber and thereby remain under pressure ready to dive again. Submersibles could deploy over the stern, and her dynamic positioning system allowed her to remain over a fixed point in the ocean. However, the 1980s were a time of austerity and the ship was deemed too much of a luxury so she was decommissioned in 1990. *(Crown Copyright/MoD)*

HMS CHARYBDIS

Built by Harland and Wolff, Belfast, and completed in 1969. She operated as Gibraltar guardship and then deployed east of Suez as part of the large RN presence in the Far East. In 1973 she was deployed off Iceland during the Cod Wars and again in 1976. From 1979-82 she underwent a modernisation refit at Devonport emerging as a Seawolf Leander. If the Ikara conversion costs were eyewatering, the Seawolf conversion ranged from £60-£80 million (still cheaper than the Type 22s then under construction). The superstructure was significantly lightened to allow for the weight of the GWS 25 system, trackers, launchers, radar and electronics. She decommissioned in 1991 and was sunk as a target in 1993. *(Crown Copyright/MoD)*

HMS CHURCHILL

Built by Vickers, Barrow, and completed in 1970, at a cost of over £24 million, she was the first of three improved Valiant class nuclear-powered submarines. She was powered by a single pressurised water-cooled reactor that provided steam to two geared-turbines, driving a single shaft. She was equipped with six 21-inch torpedo tubes mounted in the bow which were capable of firing the Mk8 and Mk24 Tigerfish torpedoes. In 1981 she became the first RN submarine to carry the Sub-Harpoon missile which was fired from the torpedo tubes in an anti-ship role. She was decommissioned in 1991 and still (2012) remains laid up afloat, at Rosyth, pending disposal. *(Crown Copyright/MoD)*

HMS CLEOPATRA

Built by HM Dockyard Devonport and completed in 1966, she joined the 2nd DS, in the Far East and then participated in the Beira Patrol. In 1973 she deployed to the Cod Wars. She underwent Exocet conversion from 1973-5. The 4.5-inch turret was replaced by four Exocet missiles and a quadruple Seacat launcher. Two further launchers were sited on the hangar roof. The Limbo well was plated over and two sets of STWS were fitted. The enlarged flightdeck meant that she could operate the Lynx helicopter. In 1982 she was fitted with a towed array which saw the forward Seacat, the Type 965 aerial and some superstructure removed to reduce topweight. She paid off in 1992 and was scrapped in 1994.   *(Crown Copyright/MoD)*

HMS CORNWALL

Built by Yarrow and completed in 1988, she was the first of the Batch III Type 22 frigates. The four ships of the class were ordered to replace losses during the Falklands War. They differed from the earlier ships by having a 4.5-inch gun forward and eight Harpoon missiles (vice 4 Exocet) mounted on the superstructure ahead of the foremast. They also mounted a single Goalkeeper CIWS. They are able to accommodate a flagstaff and have extensive command and control facilities. She operated widely east of Suez on anti-terror operations and anti-piracy patrols. In 2007 fifteen of her crew were detained by Iranian forces in the vicinity of disputed territorial waters. She decommissioned in 2011. *(Crown Copyright/MoD)*

HMS COVENTRY

Completed by Cammell Laird in 1978, her career was short but eventful. She deployed east of Suez in 1980 becoming the first RN ship in 30 years to visit China. On her return she was diverted to the Persian Gulf following the outbreak of the Iran-Iraq war. In 1982 she was part of the Falklands Task Force, becoming the first ship to fire Sea Dart in anger (initially unsuccessfully against Learjets ad later on shooting down two Skyhawks) and her helicopters the first to fire Sea Skua (against the tug ALFEREZ SOBRAL). On 25 May 1982 she was struck by three bombs entering the hull close to the waterline. She was abandoned within 20 minutes after which she rolled over and sank. 19 of her crew were lost. *(Crown Copyright/MoD)*

HMS COVENTRY

Built by Swan Hunter and commissioned in 1988 she was originally to have been named BOADICEA, but was renamed COVENTRY in order to honour the destroyer sunk during the Falklands conflict. These later Type 22 frigates incorporated many of the lessons learnt during the war. The use of structural aluminium was kept to a minimum; smoke curtains were adopted to prevent the spread of smoke; cabling was left unpainted and non-toxic varieties used and shatterproof decorative coverings were adopted throughout. She was identified as surplus to requirements following the 1998 defence cuts and paid off in 2002 being transfered to Romania and renamed REGELE FERDINAND. *(Crown Copyright/MoD)*

HMS CUMBERLAND

Built by Yarrow and completed in 1989. She was deployed to the Falklands during 1990-91. In 2003 she was on patrol in the Caribbean when she intercepted cocaine with a street value of almost £200 million. She emerged from refit in 2008 and deployed east of Suez as part of SNMG2 in support of anti-piracy operations and again in 2010 on maritime security operations in the area. As part of defence cuts she was to pay off in 2011, but continued to prove her usefulness when, on her return voyage to the UK, she diverted to Libya to evacuate entitled nationals from the country and remained on scene conducting maritime security patrols. She arrived at Devonport in April and decommissioned in June. *(Crown Copyright/MoD 1989)*

HMS CUTLASS

One of three such vessels built by Vosper Thornycroft, she was completed in 1970. Based on the design of the Brave class they were classified as Fast Training Boats and operated by the 1st FTB Squadron at Portland to train surface and airborne forces in anti-fast patrol boat tactics. Powered by two Proteus gas turbines, with diesels for cruising, they were capable of speeds of 40 knots. They were designed to accommodate a third gas turbine and could carry guns and missiles if required. The only vessel to deploy operationally was SCIMITAR which served for a while in Hong Kong on anti-Illegal Immigrant patrols. Together with her sisters she was placed on the disposal list in 1981 and bought by Greek interests. *(Crown Copyright/MoD)*

71

RFA DILIGENCE

Yet another result of the Falklands War she was formerly the oil rig support ship STENA INSPECTOR, built in 1981 by Oresundsvarvet, Sweden. She was taken up from trade (STUFT) in 1982 to provide forward repair for warships damaged during the conflict. She was purchased outright in 1983 and refitted at Clyde Dock Engineering where she had workshops, additional accommodation and military equipment fitted. She has an ice-strengthened hull and is able to operate as an HQ and support ship for both MCMVs and when necessary deployed submarines.

(Crown Copyright/MoD 1989)

HMS DIOMEDE

Built by Yarrow and completed in 1971. In 1972 took part in Second Cod War. In 1976, during Third Cod War she was rammed four times (three by ICGV BALDUR and once by ICGV TYR), causing so much damage on the fourth occasion that she had to return to th UK for repairs. Was scheduled to undergo Seawolf conversion, but this was cancelled by the 1981 defence cuts. Reducing to Standby Squadron was reprieved due to Falklands War to cover for ships deployed 'down south.' Following the war she deployed to the South Atlantic and underwent a restorative refit to keep her operational, finally paying off in 1988 and being transferred to Pakistan as SHAMSHEER.   *(Crown Copyright/MoD)*

HMS EDINBURGH

A Batch III or 'Stretched' Type 42 she was built by Cammell Laird and completed in 1985. The 'Stretched' title is a bit of a misnomer as this was the original design, the former ten 'stumpy' ships being reduced in length to 125 metres as a budgetary cut during acquisition. EDINBURGH was unique in that she was fitted with a single Phalanx CIWS forward. Despite the addition of enlarged breakwaters and a bulwark this position was too exposed and she eventually received the standard two systems either side of the funnel. The additional weight of CIWS and other new systems necessitated external hull strengthening box beams in the four Batch III ships.

(Crown Copyright/MoD)

HMS ENDURANCE

Built in Denmark in 1956 as the mercantile ANITA DAN she was acquired by the RN for operations in the Antarctic. She was converted by Harland and Wolff in 1967 being fitted with a hangar and flightdeck and a working deck forward for handling survey launches. She was deployed to the South Atlantic at the time the Falklands War broke out and took an active role in the opening moves of the campaign. Her two Wasp helicopters assisted in attacks on the submarine SANTA FE, which was later abandoned by her crew. She continued in service until 1991 until replaced by a newer vessel, the MV POLAR CIRCLE which later also carried the name of ENDURANCE in RN service.

(Crown Copyright/MoD)

RFA ENGADINE

Built by Henry Robb Ltd, Leith, she was completed in 1967 as a replacement for the converted LST LOFOTEN. She provided facilities for operational flying training. She was based, throughout her career, at Portland, but during the Falklands War was deployed to the South Atlantic, where she operated in San Carlos Water, providing helicopter support and a refuelling base. On her return she had her flightdeck extended to allow operations by Sea King helicopters. She was decommissioned in 1989 and eventually scrapped in India, following a failed commercial venture in Greece.

(Crown Copyright/MoD)

HMS EURYALUS

Built by Scotts and completed in 1964, she deployed to the Far East as leader of the 26 ES. In 1966 she operated with SNFL and by 1968 was once more east of Suez. From 1973-6 she underwent Ikara conversion at Devonport. In 1978 she was part of 2 FS at Portland. In 1981 she deployed to the Persian Gulf during the Iran-Iraq war before a further spell with SNFL in 1984. In 1986 she became leader of 1 FS. She decommissioned in 1989 and was sold, like her sister AJAX, to DML for modernisation and onward sale to an overseas operator, but this plan fell through and she was scrapped at Millom in 1990.

(Crown Copyright/MoD)

HMS EXETER

Built by Swan Hunter she was completed in 1980, the first of the Batch II Type 42 destroyers. She still retained the short hull but was fitted with the Type 1022, 992Q and 1006 radars. She was operating in the Caribbean when called forward to the Falklands to replace SHEFFIELD. During the conflict, her Sea Dart missiles accounted for three Argentine aircraft. The turquoise hull on and below the waterline (seen here) was an experimental co-polymer paint which was only available in a few non-standard colours at the time. She was placed in reserve in 2008 and decommissioned in 2009. She left Portsmouth under tow in 2011 bound for breaking up in Turkey. *(Crown Copyright/MoD)*

XSV EXPLORER

One of four P2000 training boats originally acquired for operation by the RNXS, she was built by Watercraft and completed in 1985. The task of the RNXS was to assist in evacuating major ports and dispatching larger and faster merchant vessels overseas in case of an attack on the UK. The service was disbanded in 1994 and the four vessels commissioned into the RN, since when their pennant numbers were prefixed 'P' and the black hulls painted grey. HMS EXPLORER is assigned to the Yorkshire Universities Royal Naval Unit (URNU), serving the universities of York, Hull, Sheffield and Leeds.

(Crown Copyright/MoD 1987)

HMS FARNELLA

During the Falklands War there was a requirement for minesweepers to clear the sea areas around the Falklands. The Ton class were considered unsuitable for operating in the South Atlantic. Five former stern trawlers were requisitioned (PICT, CORDELLA, FARNELLA, JUNELLA & NORTHELLA) and pressed into service as the 11th MCMS. As well as minesweeping operations the ships helped in transferring 3,000 troops and their equipment from the QE2 to CANBERRA. This picture shows FARNELLA entering Gibraltar enroute back to the UK. JUNELLA can just be seen in the background berthed on South Mole as she had a mine onboard which she was returning to the UK for examination.

(Steve Bush)

HMS FENCER

Built by Fairey Allday Marine, Southampton, and completed in 1983, to a design used by the UK Customs Service. Known as the Attacker class in RN service, the five vessels were of GRP hull construction. They operated in a training role with various University Royal Navy Units, FENCER being assigned to Southampton. The whole class was decommissioned between 1991 and 1992. All five ships were sold to the Lebanese Navy in July 1992 where FENCER was renamed JOUNIEH.

(Crown Copyright/MoD)

HMS FIFE

Built by Fairfield and completed in 1966 she was one of four County class to be fitted with the Exocet missile in place of 'B' turret. In refit during the Falklands conflict she was fitted with two triple ASW torpedo mounts and operated a Lynx helicopter rather than a Wessex III. A further refit in 1986 saw her converted to operate as a cadet training ship. The Seaslug missile launcher was removed and replaced by a deckhouse containing navigation classrooms. She was decommissioned in 1987 and sold to Chile where she was renamed BLANCO ENCALADA. During her initial refit in Chile her flightdeck was extended aft. She was decommissioned in 2003 and scrapped in 2005.

(Crown Copyright/MoD

HMS FLINTHAM

One of the few survivors of 93 Inshore Minesweepers of the Ham class, she was built by Bolson and completed in 1955. For the first nine years of her life she was kept in reserve at Hythe. When she commissioned she operated as a training tender, initially to GANGES at Shotley and then to RALEIGH at Torpoint, where new entry sailors were given their first taste of life at sea. Several Ham class were converted to Torpedo Recovery Vessels, Personnel Ferries and Degaussing Vessels - all operated by the RMAS. Most of these, by the middle of the decade, were awaiting disposal. FLINTHAM was decommissioned in 1982 and sold in 1983

(Crown Copyright/MoD)

RFA FORT GRANGE

One of a pair of ships designed to replenish warships with solid stores, fresh water and ammunition while underway. Their capability was enhanced by the addition of a large hangar and flight deck, enabling the embarkation of up to four Sea King helicopters for either stores transfer or operational ASW sorties. She was built by Scott Lithgow and entered service in 1978. She operated in both the Falklands campaign and the 1991 Gulf War. From 1997 to 2000 she was based alongside at Split in the former Yugoslavia. In 2000 she was renamed FORT ROSALIE to prevent confusion with RFA FORT GEORGE.

(Crown Copyright/MoD)

HMS FOX

These Coastal Survey ships were intended to compliment the larger Hecla class of Ocean Survey vessels. FOX was built by Brooke Marine and completed in 1968. The class were fitted with a twin rudder and twin shaft arrangement with variable-pitch propellers. They were also fitted with passive tank stabilisers to help prevent rolling. For surveying they were fitted with precise navaids, specialised echo-sounders, magnetometer and a variety of sonar and radar equipment. They could also deploy two survey boats which were carried on davits amidships. She was the first of the class to de-commission being sold to commercial interests in 1989.

(Crown Copyright/MoD 1988)

HMS GALATEA

Built by Swan Hunter and completed in 1964 and immediately stationed in the Mediterranean. She underwent an Ikara conversion from 1971-74 at Devonport. She took part in the Third Cod War with Iceland and was rammed by the ICGV BALDUR. In 1980 she deployed to the Far East and the following year entered refit at Gibraltar. This view shows the cramped flight deck with the small Wasp embarked, astern of which is a three-barreled LIMBO ASW mortar and in the stern cut out the variable depth sonar. She paid off in 1986 and two years later was towed from Portsmouth to be sunk as a target.

(Crown Copyright/MoD)

HMS GLAMORGAN

Built by Vickers-Armstrongs and completed in 1966. From 1977-79, she underwent a refit when 'B' turret was replaced by four Exocet launchers. Was part of Exercise Springtrain in 1982 and diverted to the South Atlantic for the Falklands campaign. She spent a lot of time providing naval gunfire support for the troops ashore. During one such operation in June she was struck by a land-launched Exocet missile which entered the hangar causing extensive damage and killing 13 men. She returned to the UK for permanent repairs. She decommissioned in 1986 and was transferred to the Chilean Navy as ALMIRANTE LATTORE. Decommissioned in 1996, she sank enroute to the breakers yard in 2005. *(Crown Copyright/MoD 1983)*

HMS GLASGOW

Built by Swan Hunter and commissioned in 1977, this photo gives a good view of the pre-Falklands layout of this class. The short forecastle houses the 4.5-inch gun and the twin arm Sea Dart launcher. Ship's boats were then still carried at davits either side of the funnel with triple torpedo tubes aft of that. At the stern there is a small flight deck and hangar. Most noticeable is the lack of close in weapons other than two 20mm in the bridge wings. Her aft engine room was severely damaged by a bomb during the Falklands campaign and the ship returned to the UK. The ship was placed in reserve in 2005 but brought forward while NOTTINGHAM was repaired following her grounding. She was scrapped in 2009. *(Crown Copyright/MoD)*

HMSML GLEANER

Built by VT Halmatic. Portchester, she was completed in 1983. At just under 15 meters in length and a ship's company of just 8 (2 officers and 6 ratings) she is the smallest vessel in the RN. She was designed to conduct inshore surveys along the south coast of England, though she has since surveyed all around the coastline of Great Britain and visited various ports in Europe. She is equipped with multi-beam and sidescan sonar to collect bathymetric and seabed texture data. Like all of the Survey Squadron the ships are now painted in standard naval grey. *(Crown Copyright/MoD)*

HMS GLOUCESTER

A Batch III Type 42 built by Vosper Thornycroft, Woolston, she was completed in 1985. Compared to the picture on page 88 she has the extended forecastle, providing greater magazine capacity; the ship's boats have been replaced by RIBs (in the position which would later mount the Phalanx CIWS). There are two additional 20mm mounts either side of the hangar. This Batch also incorporated a larger hangar and flightdeck. In 1991 during the Gulf War her Sea Dart intercepted and destroyed an Iraqi Silkworm missile fired from ashore. She decommissioned in 2011, being replaced by a new Type 45 destroyer.

(Crown Copyright/MoD)

RFA GOLD ROVER

Completed in 1974 at a cost of £7.7 million she was built by Swan Hunter. She stood by off Cyprus during the Turkish invasion in 1974, together with HERMES and the RFAs OLNA, OLWEN and REGENT. In 1977 she conducted trials with the civilian tanker BRITISH TAMAR to establish whether or not an RFA could fill its tanks from a commercial products tanker without the need of specialised replenishment gear, something that proved very useful during the Falklands campaign, though GOLD ROVER at that time was operating off Singapore. She has deployed as the Falkland Islands tanker on many occasions - in 1990 losing her rudder during severe South Atlantic weather! She remains in service (2012). *(Crown Copyright/MoD)*

HMS GUERNSEY

One of seven ships built for the RN by Hall, Russell of Aberdeen, following successful trials, from 1975-77, with JURA, a similar ship operated by the Scottish Fisheries Protection Agency. This class formed the backbone of the FPS, whose mission was to patrol UK fishing grounds, and also ensure the security of the British oil and gas fields in the North Sea. GUERNSEY was completed in 1977 and decommissioned in 2003. She was transferred to Bangladesh the following year and was renamed BNS SANGU.

(Crown Copyright/MoD)

HMS HART

In 1985 the RAF Marine Craft Unit at Gibraltar was withdrawn and the Royal Navy Gibraltar Squadron formed to provide protection and surveillance of merchant and Soviet shipping in the Strait of Gibraltar. Two of the original RAF craft stationed at Gibraltar, HMAFV STIRLING and SUNDERLAND, were transferred to the RN and renamed HART and CORMORANT. HART is seen here, still sporting her RAF colours when operated as a Rescue and Target Towing Launch (RTTL). Both vessels were withdrawn in 1991 when they were replaced by the P2000 class patrol boats RANGER and TRUMPETER.

(Crown Copyright/MoD)

HMS HECLA

She was the lead ship of a class of three such oceangoing survey ships ordered for the RN in the mid 1960s, along with her sisters ships HECATE and HYDRA. She was built by Yarrow and completed in 1965. Able to operate for long periods away from shore support these ships were deployed worldwide to collect hydrographic data to produce Admiralty charts. In 1982 she was rapidly converted to operate as an ambulance ship during the Falklands War, supporting the hospital ships by transferring casualties from the hospital ship for repatriation to the UK, via Montivideo. She is seen here leaving Gibraltar at the end of the war on her return to the UK. She decommissioned in 1997. *(Steve Bush)*

HMS HERALD

She was a follow-on to the successful Hecla class, being very similar in appearance, but slightly larger. She was built by Robb Caledon, Leith, and completed in 1974. The most noticeable external difference were the boat davits abeam the hangar (compare with previous page). This class had an ice strengthened hull. She also deployed as an ambulance ship in 1982 and saw further service in the Falklands when she deployed as a patrol vessel while ENDURANCE was in refit. For this role she was painted grey and armed with 20mm cannon. She also operated during the Gulf War as an MCM support ship. She decommissioned in 2001 and saw commercial service as SOMERVILLE operating from Ireland. *(Crown Copyright/MoD)*

HMS HERMES

Built by Vickers she was laid down during the Second World War, but not completed until 1950. She served, mainly in the Far East as a conventional aircraft carrier, until 1971 when she was converted to a Commando Carrier and again in 1976 to an ASW carrier. In 1980 she was fitted with a ski-jump to enable her to operate the Sea Harrier. She was to be decommissioned in 1982 but she won a reprieve, serving as flagship of the 1982 Falklands Task Force deployed to retake the islands. She entered reserve in 1984 and was paid off in 1985. In 1986 she was sold to India and refitted at Devonport. She commissioned as INS VIRAAT and remains in service (2012). *(Crown Copyright/MoD)*

HMS HERMIONE

Launched by Alex Stephen in 1967 and completed by Yarrow in 1969. She was a Broad-beam Leander, two feet wider in the beam than earlier groups. Deployed to the Far East in the 1970s. In 1978 had spent almost eight months on the Canadian and US Pacific coast. She was given a Seawolf modernisation refit at Chatham 1979-83. She sailed from Chatham after her refit, the last RN vessel to leave the dockyard before it closed. In this view the reduced superstructure aft of the foremast is evident - including the lack of a funnel cap, and an additional 20mm gun has been placed on a bandstand aft. She paid off in 1992 and was towed away for breaking up in India in 1998. *(Crown Copyright/MoD)*

NAVAL HOVERCRAFT TRIALS UNIT

The Naval Hovercraft Trials Unit was formed in 1975 following the disbandment of the Interservice Hovercraft Trials Unit which had formed in 1962. Over the years the unit operated several types of hovercraft for evaluation including the small SRN6 (bottom), the BH7 (centre) and the large VT2 (top). Many possible uses were envisioned, including minesweeping, offshore patrol, troop carrying and missile craft. Although trials took place through to the middle of the 1980s, the hovercraft remained a novelty, although the SRN 6 did see operations off Hong Kong on Illegal Immigrant patrols. *(Crown Copyright/MoD)*

HMS HUBBERSTON

She was competed in 1955 having been built by Fleetlands Shipyard, Gosport, although she didn't commission until the end of 1964. Throughout the 1960s she served in the Far East, initially at Singapore with the 11th MSS and then latterly with the 6th MCMS at Hong Kong, transferring to the 6th PBS at Hong Kong in 1969. She served with 2 MCMS at Portsmouth from 1972, transferring to 3 MCMS in 1989. She collided with her sister ship IVESTON that same year and was decommissioned in 1991, being broken up in Belgium from 1992.

(Crown Copyright/MoD)

HMS HURWORTH

Built by Vosper Thornycroft and completed in 1985, this Hunt class MCMV is seen here with additional 20mm guns either side of the funnel and commercial communications satellite dome forward of the sweep deck. Eight of the Hunt class served in the Persian Gulf during Operation Granby and accounted for clearing over 200 mines. When deployed to high threat areas the ships can be equipped with additional 20mm guns, decoy rocket launchers, ESM and extra communications gear. The original World War II vintage 40mm/60 cal Mk9 gun mounts have been replaced by stabilised DS-30B 30mm mounts. In 2012 only eight hunts remained in service. *(Crown Copyright/MoD 1988)*

HMS HYDRA

Built by Yarrow and completed in 1966 she was the third of the original Hecla class to enter service. They were, some-what controversially, built to a merchant ship design with good accommodation and endurance. They were fitted with a flightdeck and hangar, able to embark and operate a Wasp helicopter. There was also a garage for a Land-Rover. Deployed in 1982 as an Ambulance Ship during the Falklands War and in 1986 was involved in the evacuation of British nationals from the Yemen. She was decommissioned later that year and transferred to the Indonesian Navy and renamed DEWA KEMBAR.

(Crown Copyright/MoD 1991)

HMS ILLUSTRIOUS

The second of the three Invincible class to enter service she was built by Swan Hunter and, due to the Falklands War her completion was brought forward to 1982. She was too late to see active service but was able to relieve INVINCIBLE and remain in the area providing air defence until such time as the runway at Port Stanley was able to accommodate fighter aircraft. On her return to the UK she conducted a proper shakedown and an official commissioning ceremony. She was laid up in reserve from 1989-93. She then emerged from refit with an extended flight deck and able to switch roles between strike carrier or amphibious helicopter carrier. She is not scheduled to decommission until 2014. *(Crown Copyright/MoD 1986)*

HMS INTREPID

The second of two LPDs operated by the RN at the time, she was built by John Brown & Company on the Clyde and completed in 1967. Designed to transport and land Royal Marines and their equipment by both landing craft and helicopter and then remain in the area to provide command and control of operations afloat and ashore. At the outbreak of the Falklands War, the ship was in the process of destoring ready for disposal. With her sister-ship FEARLESS, they were key to the success of the operation and she was rapidly returned to service. Post war she operated as a training ship for young officers before entering reserve in 1991 and paying off in 1999. She was scrapped in Liverpool in 2008.   *(Crown Copyright/MoD)*

HMS INVINCIBLE

Built by Vickers, Barrow, she was completed in 1980. Following the 1981 defence cuts she was to have been sold to Australia, but the Falklands War demonstrated how useful she was, together with HERMES, providing air defence above the fleet and the troops ashore. She is seen here returning to Portsmouth from the South Atlantic, despite repeated claims by Argentina that she had been sunk during the conflict. Note the captured Argentine artillery pieces at the end of the flight deck. From 1993-5 she was deployed to the Adriatic on Operation Deny Flight and from 1998-9 Operation Bolton in Southern Iraq. In 2005 she was laid up, never to return to service. She was scrapped in Turkey in 2011. *(Crown Copyright/MoD 1982)*

HMS JUNO

Built by J.I. Thornycroft, Woolston, and completed in 1967. In her early career she undertook a world cruise and took part in the Beira patrol. She took part in two patrols during the Third Cod War, and on both occasions was rammed by ICGV TYR. She was to have undergone an Exocet conversion, but with costs rising to £60 million she was paid off into the Standby Squadron. In 1981 she was moved to Rosyth for conversion to a training ship. Her main armament was removed and the LIMBO well plated over. The space vacated below decks was made into classrooms. She re-entered service in 1985. She de-commissioned in 1992 and was scrapped in 1995. Compare her superstructure with that on page 97.   *(Crown Copyright/MoD)*

HMS KELLINGTON
Built by William Pickersgill & Co Ltd of Sunderland, she was completed in 1955. She commissioned in 1956 as part of the 108th MSS at Malta, but by the middle of 1956, was back in the UK and reduced to reserve at Hythe. She recommissioned in 1969 as part of the FPS until transferring to Sussex RNR in 1976. In 1985 she joined 3 MCMS at Portsmouth. Her final operational role was with the FPS from 1989-92. Paid off that year, she saw further service as a Sea Cadet HQ ship at Stockton-on-Tees, but her deteriorating material state saw her broken up in situ in 2009.

(Crown Copyright/MoD)

HMS KINGFISHER

Based on the RAF Seal class LRRV these craft were built for fishery protection duties. KINGFISHER was built by R. Dunston of Hessle and completed in 1975. They were not very successful and proved to be bad seaboats and unsuitable for the year-round fishery protection role. She was converted for coastal patrol duties with the Northern Ireland Squadron together with CYGNET and REDPOLE, being fitted with an enclosed bridge, the 40mm gun was removed and a small boat handling crane and RIB placed on the quarterdeck. Boat handling booms were fitted to the hull and the vessel was painted dark grey. She was decommissioned in 1994 and sold to a private concern in 1996.   *(Crown Copyright/MoD 1987)*

HMS LEANDER

The nameship of her class, she was originally laid down, by Harland and Wolff, as the Type 12 frigate WEYMOUTH, being completed as LEANDER in 1963. In 1964 she joined the forerunner of SNFL, Matchmaker I. From 1970-72 she was converted, at Devonport, to carry the Ikara missile system. She took part in the Third Cod Wars and was rammed by ICGV THOR in January 1976, causing such serious damage, that she had to return to the UK for repairs. During the transit she broke down in severe gales and was escorted back by BACCHANTE. She paid off into the Standby Squadron in 1986 and sunk as a target in 1989.

(Crown Copyright/MoD)

HMS LEEDS CASTLE

Built by Hall Russell of Aberdeen, the two Castle class vessels were laid down as a speculative venture as an Offshore Patrol vessel. Completed in 1981 and purchased by the MoD while building, she had a dual role of Fishery Protection and Offshore Patrol and Surveillance. Armament was limited to a 40mm Bofors (latter a 30mm Bmarc) but, unlike the Island class, the Castles were fitted with a flightdeck that could land and refuel helicopters up to Sea King size. She participated in the Falklands War in 1982 and shared the task of Falkland Island Patrol Vessel with her sister. She decommissioned in 2005 and, together with her sister, was sold to Bangladesh in 2010 and renamed DHALESHWARI. *(Crown Copyright/MoD)*

HMS LINDESFARNE

Built by Hall Russell of Aberdeen she was completed in 1978. These vessels were based on a trawler hull and were armed with a single 40mm gun ahead of the bridge. The quarterdeck was given over to boat operations with handling cranes and two RIBs for conducting boardings and inspections. Diesel-powered with a single shaft the ships had a range of 11,000 nm at 11 knots. LINDESFARNE was decommissioned in 2003 and transferred to Bangladesh the following year where she was renamed BNS TURAG. *(Crown Copyright/MoD)*

HMS LIVERPOOL

Built by Cammell Laird with her completion accelerated due to the Falklands War. She was accepted in May 1982 and after an abbreviated trials programme deployed to the South Atlantic in June. She arrived too late to see action, but remained on station for the following six months. She operated in the Mediterranean with NATO forces on Operation Active Endeavour and was diverted from a Far East deployment in 2003 for operations against Iraq. In the twilight of her career in 2011 she was on active operations again, this time off Libya during the Arab Spring, becoming the first RN vessel in over 30 years to come under fire. On her return she conducted a few UK port visits prior to decommissioning in 2012. *(Crown Copyright/MoD)*

HMS LONDON

Built by Yarrow and completed in 1987, she was to have been named BLOODHOUND, but was one of three Type 22 frigates renamed in the wake of the Falklands War. In this view the enlarged flight deck and the taller hangar, slightly offset to port, can be seen. On the stern, the large round fairlead seen on the port quarter is from where the towed array was streamed. The Batch II frigates in particular spent a lot of time on ASW TA patrols in the vicinity of the GIUK gap often in rough seas and often a problem for aircraft in the hangar, the door of which was susceptible to damage in following seas. LONDON was decommissioned in 1999 and sold to Romania and renamed REGINA MARIA.   *(Crown Copyright/MoD)*

HMS LONDONDERRY

A Type 12 frigate, she was built by J. Samuel White & Co. Ltd and completed in 1962. Following service in the West Indies and Far East, she underwent modernisation at Portsmouth from 1967-69, emerging with a flightdeck and hangar which enabled her to operate a Wasp helicopter. Between 1975 and 1979 she was refitted at Rosyth for service as a trials ship for ASWE. She had her armament removed and additional masts and deckhouses fitted for trialling various radars. She arrived at Portsmouth to pay-off in March 1982, but was reprieved due to the Falklands War. She went on to serve as the Dartmouth Training Ship until finally decommissioning in 1984. *(Crown Copyright/MoD)*

HMS LOWESTOFT

Built by Alex Stephen and completed in 1961. She was the first ship on the Beira patrol in 1966 - an operation to blockade oil shipments to Rhodesia (now Zimbabwe) through Beira, Mozambique. She underwent a reconstruction refit at Chatham to allow her to operate a helicopter from 1967-70. From 1976-77 she was converted at Portsmouth to undertake trials with the new towed-array sonar, the equipment being housed on the flightdeck and quarterdeck. She was restored to operations post Falklands, but decommissioned in 1985 and was sunk as a target in 1986.

(Crown Copyright/MoD)

HMS LOYAL WATCHER

A large number of fleet tenders were built from 1971 for support duties and goods or personnel transfer, both within the naval bases and to support ships around the coast. Similar vessels were acquired as diving support vessels, while others were operated by the RNXS on port protection operations. Most were operated by the RMAS but some variants saw service under the White Ensign. LOYAL WATCHER was originally operated by the RNXS, but saw service with the RN as a URNU vessel. Four further vessels, MANLY, MENTOR, MILBROOK and MESSINA were completed in 1982 as training vessels for new entry sailors and Royal Marines, with classrooms rather than holds.   *(Crown Copyright/MoD)*

HMS MANCHESTER

Built by Vickers and completed in 1982. She was part of the Global 86 deployment and two years later was deployed to the Persian Gulf as part of the Armilla Patrol. In 1991 she deployed to the area again in support of the first Gulf War, following Iraq's invasion of Kuwait. Nicknamed the 'Busy Bee' her final deployment was in 2010 to the Caribbean where she became the first RN warship to visit Cuba since the Castro revolution. During the seven months deployed she conducted counter drugs operations and provided humanitarian relief to the hurricane ravaged island of St. Lucia. She was decommissioned in 2011.

(Crown Copyright/MoD 1986)

HMS MINERVA

Built by Vickers Armstrong and completed in 1966. In 1967 she served in the Far East, and a year later was on the West Indies station. In 1973 she again sailed for the Caribbean, this time with HRH The Prince of Wales on board for training. She underwent Exocet conversion at Chatham from 1975-79 (she suffered a boiler explosion during post refit trials in 1978 and had to return to dock for repairs). She is seen here in the original Exocet standard, with the third Seacat launcher forward and the Exocet mounted on a raised deck with blast deflectors aft and two 40mm above the bridge wings. She paid off in 1992 and was towed to India for breaking up in 1993. *(Crown Copyright/MoD)*

P1055

HMS MONKTON

Having been built by Herd & Mackenzie, Buckie, it was to be over two years from completion before she was eventually commissioned in 1959 to serve with the Vernon Training Squadron (renamed 5 MSS in 1962) at Portsmouth. She transferred to 1 MCMS at Port Edgar in 1965, prior to entering refit at Devonport in 1971 for conversion to a patrol craft. Renumbered from M1155 to P1055 she operated as part of the HKPS between 1972-85, when she paid off. She was sold and broken up locally in Hong Kong.

(Crown Copyright/MoD)

HMS NAIAD

Built by Yarrow, Scotstoun (the 200th vessel built by the yard for the RN) and completed in 1965. She was the first Leander class frigate to receive the Seacat missile system from build. Between 1973-75 she underwent an Ikara conversion at Devonport. She was rammed by the ICGV TYR during the Third Cod War, requiring repairs at Devonport. She was scheduled for disposal in 1981 but retained to cover for ships deployed to the Falklands. She paid off in 1987. Renamed HULVUL, between 1988-90 she underwent shock, fire and blast trials and was used to analyse developments in weapons and ship technology learnt from the Falklands Conflict. She was finally sunk in 1990 as a target. *(Crown Copyright/MoD)*

HMS NEWCASTLE
Built by Swan Hunters and completed in 1978 the ship is seen here in her original guise, pre-Falkands enhancements. The black band on the funnel indicates that she is half-leader to the 6th DS. Note the Type 909 trackers. The radomes were sometimes removed post refit or during calibration serials to allow access to the trackers. Known throughout the fleet as the "Geordie Gunboat' she operated in the South Atlantic, Mediterranean and West Indies, and in 1992 was part of the Global 1992 deployment. In 1988 she was unfortunate enough to be damaged when hit in the engine room by a target she had just engaged with her CIWS. She was decommissioned in 2005 and broken up in Turkey in 2008   . *(Crown Copyright/MoD)*

HMS NOTTINGHAM

She was commissioned in 1983, having been built by Vosper Thornycroft at Woolston. Compared to the picture of her sistership on the previous page, she is fitted with the Type 1022 radar and the full CIWS fit received post 1982. She served in both the Gulf and Adriatic and underwent an extensive modernisation refit in 2000 to extend her service life to 2012. However, in July 2002, she ran aground 200 miles off the coast of Australia. A 160 ft hole was torn in the hull, flooding five compartments. Good damage control procedures saved the ship and she was returned to the UK aboard a heavylift ship for repair (costing £39 million) and return to service (July 2004). She decommissioned in 2010. *(Crown Copyright/MoD)*

RFA OAKLEAF

Built by A B Uddevalla, Sweden she was launched in 1981 as OKTANIA. She was acquired by MoD, under bare-boat charter in 1986 and renamed OAKLEAF. At 48,000 tons she was the largest tanker in service with the RFA at the time. She was fitted with a single RAS rig for abeam refuelling and had a deck space forward of the bridge for containers to support long deployments. She spent much of her operational career in support of warships deployed to the Caribbean. She was decommissioned in 2007 and towed to Aliaga, Turkey, for breaking up in 2010.   *(Crown Copyright/MoD)*

HMS OBERON

She was the lead boat of a new class of diesel-powered submarines, a direct development of the earlier Porpoise class. Changes were primarily to improve the strength and stealth of the submarine. The hull was built from QT28 steel (vice UXW), which was easier to fabricate and stronger, allowing the submarine to dive deeper. GRP was used in construction of the casing. She was built by HM Dockyard Chatham and completed in 1961. Proving to be a very successful design, thirteen were built for the RN, with a further fourteen serving with four overseas navies. She decommissioned in 1986 and broken up at Grimsby in 1991 following a failed transfer to the Egyptian Navy. *(Crown Copyright/MoD)*

RFA OLWEN

A development of the Improved Tide Class fleet tankers, the three "Ol' class vessels were the fastest in the RFA fleet. Laid down in 1963 by Hawthorne Leslie, she was completed in 1965. She was originally named OLYNTHUS but this was subsequently changed in 1967 to avoid confusion with the submarine OLYMPUS. Of 36,000 tons the ships carried a wide range of fuel, aviation spirits and lubricants, in addition to limited dry stores. They had a flightdeck and a hangar which could accommodate up to three large helicopters. She was decommissioned in 1999 and broken up in India in 2001.

(Crown Copyright/MoD)

HMS ONSLAUGHT

Built by HM Dockyard Chatham and completed in 1962, she was the first RN submarine to bear the name. These submarines were fitted with eight torpedo tubes (6 bow and 2 stern) and could carry 30 torpedoes. They had a submerged speed of 17 knots and 12 knots on the surface, using diesel electric propulsion. The submarines were equipped with a Type 1002 surface search and navigation radar, a Type 187 Active-Passive attack sonar, and a Type 2007 long range passive sonar, replaced in some vessels by the Type 2051. ONSLAUGHT was paid off in 1990 and towed to Turkey for breaking up in 1991.

(Crown Copyright/MoD)

RFA ORANGELEAF

She was built by Cammell Laird and launched in 1975 as HUDSON PROGRESS, but not taken over by her owners due to financial difficulties. In May 1982 she was requisitioned, as BALDER LONDON, for service during the Falklands conflict. Two years laters she was bareboat chartered by the MoD for operation by the RFA and renamed ORANGE-LEAF. She underwent conversion at Falmouth and the Tyne before entering service in 1986. She supported ARK ROYAL on Outback 88 and took part in both Gulf Wars. She regularly assumes the role of FOST tanker for sea train-ing serials and (in 2012) remains the only Leaf class still in service. *(Crown Copyright/MoD 1988)*

HMS PEACOCK

Five of this class were ordered in 1981 to replace the elderly Ton class operating with the Hong Kong Patrol Squadron. Built by Hall Russell and completed in 1983, the ships were 75% funded by the Government of Hong Kong. PEACOCK was the first RN vessel to be armed with the Oto Melara 76mm Compact gun. Diesel powered she had two Sea Rider boarding craft on her quarterdeck. Two of the ships (SWIFT and SWALLOW) were sold to Ireland in 1988. In 1997, after Hong Kong was ceded back to China, the remaining three vessels were transferred to the Philippines with PEACOCK being renamed EMILIO JACINTO.

(Crown Copyright/MoD)

HMS PENELOPE

Built by Vickers Armstrong and completed in 1963 she initially operated with 20 FS at Londonderry. In 1966 she entered refit at Devonport, emerging in 1967 as a trials ship for AUWE investigating hull noise created by warships. She was later used as the Seawolf trials ship, with a launcher and deckhouse fitted on the flightdeck. From 1977-81 she underwent Exocet conversion and sailed to the Falkands, with the BRISTOL reinforcement group, in 1982. Between 1983-85 the ship made a further four deployments to the region. In 1988 she collided with HMCS PRESERVER requiring four months of repairs. Paid off in 1991 and transfered to Ecuador as PRESIDENTE ELOY ALFARO. *(Crown Copyright/MoD)*

HMS PHOEBE

Built by Alex Stephen and completed in 1966. She assisted in the withdrawal from Aden in 1967 and two years later took part in the 20th Anniversary of NATO Fleet Review held at Spithead. She took part in the Second Cod War and from 1973 was periodically used for the filming of the popular BBC TV drama *Warship*, set on board the fictional HMS HERO. She underwent Exocet conversion at Devonport from 1975-77. In 1977-8 she led a Task Group to the Falklands as a show of force to quell Argentine rhetoric. She was fitted with towed array from 1982-4, eventually mounted on a sponson offset over the starboard quarter. She paid off in 1990 and was towed to India in 1992 for breaking up. *(Crown Copyright/MoD)*

RFA PLUMLEAF

One of eight vessels acquired from civilian owners during the 1960s for freighting duties, she was laid down in 1958 at Blyth Drydock and Engineering Co. On completion in 1960 she was chartered by the MoD and named PLUMLEAF. In 1966 she was fitted with a replenishment rig. In 1982 she was part of Exercise Springtrain at Gibraltar, preparing for a Far East deployment. She was quickly retasked to support vessels sailing from the UK to Ascension Island and for the following months took station between Ascension and the Falklands as one of four tankers in the 'motorway chain' providing fuel to TF ships, conducting 55 RAS serials and transfering 19,523 tonnes of fuel. She paid off in 1986. *(Crown Copyright/MoD 1979)*

HMS PLYMOUTH

Completed by HM Dockyard Devonport in 1961. During the Falklands War she was detached from the main Task Group with ANTRIM, BRILLIANT and ENDURANCE for Operation Paraquet, the action to recapture South Georgia. On 8 June during an air raid over San Carlos Water she was hit by four bombs, one hitting the flight deck, detonating a depth charge and starting a fire, one going straight through the funnel and two more destroying her Limbo AS mortar. She decommissioned in 1988 and was preserved as a museum from 1989-2006, though, at the time of going to press her future is now uncertain.

(Crown Copyright/MoD)

HMS PURSUER

One of sixteen P2000 training vessels operated by the RN, PURSUER was completed in 1988. Based on a design for an Omani Coastguard cutter 12 were built for the RN with a further four for the RNXS, but subsequently transferred to the RN. All vessels constitute the 1st PBS. Originally assigned to Sussex University, in 2003 she was deployed to the Mediterranean to form the Cyprus Squadron in support of Operation Telic and armed with up to 3 GPMGs. In 2010 she returned to the UK to form part of the Faslane Patrol Boat Squadron (FPBS) at HMNB Clyde where she provides security patrols and escort duties to the deterrent submarines. She has been fitted with armour around the bridge. *(Crown Copyright/MoD)*

RFA REGENT

Built by Harland and Wolff and completed in 1967, she was one of a pair of Admiralty designed Ammunition ships, capable of carrying the full range of naval ammunition and armament stores, together with limited naval stores and provisions. They were the first RFA's to be allocated permanent Flights and carried Wessex HU5 helicopters until April 1987 when the Wessex was withdrawn from service. In 1982 she supported Operation Corporate - the deployment to retake the Falkland Islands, returning to the UK in September that year. She participated in the first Gulf War, supporting the ARK ROYAL Group and was placed on the disposal list in 1992. She was broken up at Alang, India, in 1993.   *(Crown Copyright/MoD 1988)*

HMS RESOLUTION

Built by Vickers-Armstrong and completed in 1967 she was the first RN submarine to have an inter-continental ballistic nuclear missile capability, in this case, sixteen Polaris missiles. Together with her three sisters, they provided the UKs nuclear deterrent until replaced by the Vanguard class with the Trident missile in the 1990s. RESOLUTION had her missiles upgraded to A3 standard, with Chevaline warheads in 1984. She completed 60 patrols and was paid off in 1994, having run on an extra few months due to delays with the Vanguard class. As with all ex-RN nuclear-powered submarines, she remains laid up afloat at Rosyth until a decision is made about her future disposal.

(Crown Copyright/MoD)

RFA RESOURCE

She was completed in 1967 by Scotts Shipbuilding and Engineering, Greenock. One of her first duties was to take part in the Western Fleet Review in Torbay in 1969. She took part in operations off Aden, Cyprus and Rhodesia before supporting the Falklands Task Force. She remained at anchor in San Carlos Water during some of the fiercest air raids and emerged unscathed - despite being full of ammunition. Between 1992-1997 she operated alongside in Croatia in support of British Forces in that country. She decommissioned in 1997 and that same year left the UK for breaking up in India.

(Crown Copyright/MoD)

HMS ROEBUCK

Built by Brooke Marine, Lowestoft, and completed in 1986, she was an improved version of the earlier Fox class coastal survey vessel. Although nominally a survey vessel she could (and did) act as a support ship for mine warfare vessels. Her military role was further enhanced when tasked with conducting route surveys for potential landing sites for amphibious operations. As such she was armed with a 20mm BMARC gun and her paint scheme changed to the traditional grey of a warship. She took part in the Gulf War in 2003 and was the first RN ship into Umm Qasr following the war. She received a SLEP to see her through to 2014, but was decommissioned in 2010 and sold to Bangladesh. *(Crown Copyright/MoD 1987)*

HMS ROTHESAY

Built by Yarrow and completed in 1960, she was the lead ship of the Improved Type 12 class and the first to undergo modernisation (at Rosyth 1966-68). She undertook Cod War patrols in 1973 and a Gulf Patrol in 1981. She was unavailable for the Falklands War, being under repair, but on completion deployed to the Caribbean. Note the post-Falklands all-over grey scheme, including ships boats masts and funnel caps. It was to be toward the end of the first decade of the 21st century before black funnel tops began to re-appear. In 1985 she was refitted to operate as Dartmouth Training Ship. She paid off in 1988 and was towed to Spain later that year for breaking up.

(Crown Copyright/MoD)

HMS SANDOWN

Built by Vosper Thornycroft and commissioned in 1989 she was the first of an eventual class of twelve Single Role Mine-hunters built for the RN. Built of GRP they were designed to detect, classify and destroy mines using onboard sonar and remote vehicles. In 1999 she was involved in operations to rid the Adriatic of ordnance following the break up of Yugoslavia and in 2003 cleared mines in the Gulf after Operation Telic. She was decommissioned early in 2005 and a year later was sold to Estonia where she was renamed ADMIRAL COWAN.   *(Crown Copyright/MoD)*

HMS SANDPIPER

Built by R. Dunston of Hessle she was completed in 1977. They were a controversial acquisition, being several years late. costing £1.1 million each and proving unsatisfactory in the fishery protection role for which they were acquired. All subsequently were converted for alternative roles, SANDPIPER and PETEREL being assigned to Britannia Royal Naval College for use a training vessels. They were fitted with an enclosed bridge, but unlike the Northern Ireland Squadron, retained their 40mm gun on the quarterdeck. She was sold in 1991 to C&H Heuvelmann Shipping and Trading (Holland) for resale at Rotterdam.

(Crown Copyright/MoD)

SEAFORTH CLANSMAN

With the elderly RECLAIM having paid off and a new Diving Ship yet to complete, there was a requirement to find a vessel to maintain the RNs deep diving capability and to cover the gap for the short term. SEAFORTH CLANSMAN was built by Cochranes and completed in 1977 for Seaforth Marine Ltd and chartered for use by the RN. She was equipped with firefighting and anti-pollution gear, but more importantly a moonpool and stern gantry for diving and submersible operations. Manned by Naval Party 1007 her most notable operation was the recovery of the world's first submarine HOLLAND 1 which had been discovered off the south coast of the UK.

(Seaforth Marine)

HMS SENTINEL

Built by Husumwerft as the commercial oil-rig support vessel SEAFORTH WARRIOR, and completed in 1975, she was purchased in 1983, together with two similar vessels SEAFORTH CHAMPION and SEAFORTH SAGA (which became GUARDIAN and PROTECTOR), to operate as Falkland Islands Patrol Vessels. She was refitted for the role at Cardiff and commissioned as SENTINEL in 1984, armed with two 40mm guns and equipped with two RIBs for boarding operations. While the remaining pair were paid off in 1986, SENTINEL was retained and employed as a submarine support and security vessel on the Clyde. She decommissioned in 1992.

(Crown Copyright/MoD)

HMS SHEFFIELD

The first of the Type 42 destroyers to enter service, she was built by Vickers, Barrow and commissioned in 1975. She was unique in having 'mickey mouse ear' exhausts either side of the funnel. The ship was part of the Falkland Islands Task Force sent south in 1982. On 4 May she was hit by an air-launched Exocet anti-ship missile from a Super Etendard aircraft belonging to the Argentine Navy. Although the missile failed to explode, the rocket fuel started extensive fires and as the firemain had been breached, firefighting efforts were unsuccessful and the ship was abandoned and taken in tow by YARMOUTH towards the repair ship anchorage (TRALA) however she foundered on 10 May. *(Crown Copyright/MoD)*

HMS SHEFFIELD

Originally to have been named BRUISER, she was renamed to honour the ship lost in the Falklands War. Built by Swan Hunter she was completed in 1988 as a Batch II Type 22 frigate. Traditionally known throughout the fleet as the 'Shiny Sheff' due to the amount of stainless steel fittings donated by the city of Sheffield, she saw operations in the Mediterranean, Adriatic, Gulf and Caribbean. In 1998 she was awarded the Wilkinson Sword of Peace for providing humanitarian assistance to Nicaragua and Honduras after Hurricane Mitch. She decommissioned in 2002 and was sold to Chile in 2003 and renamed ALMIRANTE WILLIAMS.

(Crown Copyright/MoD)

HMS SHERATON

A product of Whites Shipyard, Southampton, she was completed in 1956 and commissioned for the first time in 1959. In 1964 she entered refit for conversion to a minehunter, recommissioning in 1965 at Portsmouth. She was assigned to the 6th MCMS, operating in the Far East until returning to the UK in 1972, where she joined the 1st MCMS. There followed (1980-82) an extended refit at Gibraltar, following which there was further service with 1 MCMS at Port Edgar. In 1984 she joined the 3rd MCMS at Rosyth and finished her naval service on loan to FPS (1991-93). She was scrapped in 1998.

(Crown Copyright/MoD)

HMS SHETLAND

Laid down in 1975 by Hall, Russell in Aberdeen she was launched on 22 October 1976 and commissioned on 14 July 1977. Initially the ships had a tendency to roll in heavy weather. To cut down this motion the ships were fitted with enlarged bilge keels, while the final ships built were fitted with stabilisers. In 1992, while patrolling the North Sea, she intercepted a British-registered oil rig support vessel, and seized £30 million worth of cocaine. She decommissioned in 2002 and was transferred to the Bangladesh Navy in 2003 and renamed KAPATAKHAYA. *(Crown Copyright/MoD 1978)*

RFA SIR BEDIVERE

Built by Hawthorne Leslie, Hebburn and completed in 1967 she was initially placed under the management of British India Steam Navigation Co Ltd, London before being transferred to the RFA in 1970. In 1972 she was part of a British Amphibious Task Force patrolling off British Honduras to provide an anti-invasion force. She took part in the Falklands War in 1982 and between 1994-97 underwent a SLEP at Rosyth that involved cutting the ship in half to insert an extension and a complete rebuild of her superstructure. The conversion was so expensive that she was to be the only one completed. She was decommissioned in 2008 and sold to Brazil and renamed ALMIRANTE SABOIA. *(Crown Copyright/MoD 1990)*

RFA SIR CARADOC

Following the Falklands War, there was a requirement for a Ro-Ro vessel to replace RFA SIR TRISTRAM which was severely damaged following an Argentine bombing raid on Bluff Cove on 8 June 1982 (*see page 151*). She was returned to the UK for repairs, but in the interim MV GREY MASTER, a Norwegian built vessel, was chartered from March 1983 and renamed SIR CARADOC in RFA service. Found to be unsuitable for the South Atlantic she was primarily operated on the Marchwood to Antwerp freigt run. Her charter was ended in 1988 and she was handed over to new Norwegian owners.

(Crown Copyright/MoD)

RFA SIR GALAHAD (II)

She was ordered in 1984 as a replacement for the earlier ship of the same name which had been sunk as a War Grave after the 1982 Falklands Conflict. Built by Swan Hunter, she was completed in 1987 at a cost of £40 million. She differed from her earlier sisters (*see opposite*) in having a visor style bow door, increased capacity cranes and an updated superstructure. She served in both the Gulf Wars (Operation Granby 1991 and Operation Telic 2003) and was the first vessel to bring humanitarian aid to Umm Qasr after the war. She paid off in 2006 and was sold to Brazil. being renamed GARCIA D'AVILA.

(Crown Copyright/MoD)

RFA SIR GERAINT

The fourth LSL to be laid down, she was built by Alexander Stephen, Linthouse, and completed in 1967. In April 1982 she sailed from Devonport with 450 Royal Marines and 3 Gazelle helicopters embarked. She joined the Amphibious Landing Group comprising SIR LANCELOT, SIR PERCIVALE, SIR GALAHAD, SIR TRISTRAM and PEARLEAF bound for the Falklands War. In 1997 she participated in the Ocean Wave 97 deployment to the Far East and in 2000 was supporting British forces in Sierra Leone as part of Operation Palliser. She paid off in 2003 and was scrapped in Pakistan in 2005.

(Crown Copyright/MoD)

RFA SIR LAMORAK
A second Ro-Ro vessel chartered after the Falklands War, this time to cover the loss of SIR GALAHAD (*see page 148*). She was built by Ankerlokken in Norway and completed in 1972. When chartered in 1983 she was named LAKESPAN ONTARIO, but was renamed SIR LAMORAK in RFA service, perpetuating the Knights of the Round Table names for the RFA Ro-Ro's. As with SIR CARADOC, due to stability problems, she was unsuitable for operations in the South Atlantic and was restricted to European freighting operations. Her charter expired in 1986 and she was returned to her owners.

(Crown Copyright/MoD)

RFA SIR TRISTRAM

Built by Hawthorne Leslie, Hebburn and completed in 1967. On June 1982 she was bombed and extensively damaged in Bluff Cove. She was hit by three bombs which caused extensive damage to the after part of the ship. Due to the large fires and exploding ammunition the ship was abandoned. She was moved to Port Stanley and used as an accommodation hulk before being returned to the UK for rebuilding (1984-85). She went on to serve during the first Gulf War, off Sierra Leone and humanitarian operations in the Caribbean (for which she received the Wilkinson Sword of Peace). She paid off in 2006 and today serves, as a static training ship for maritime special forces, in Portland Harbour. *(Crown Copyright/MoD 1988)*

HMS SIRIUS

Built by HM Dockyard Portsmouth and completed in 1966, the last warship to be built at the yard until HMS TYNE in 2003. In 1967 she deployed to the Pacific and Far East and was present at Tonga for the Coronation of Taufa'ahau Tupou IV. In 1970 she was awarded the Wilkinson Sword of Peace following the rescue of 100 survivors and the harrowing recovery of hundreds of bodies following the St Kitts ferry disaster. She was fitted with the Exocet missile system from 1975-7 and towed array from 1981-3. Compare this view, with enlarged flightdeck, torpedo tubes and Lynx helicopter with the Ikara conversion on page 119. She was paid off in 1993 and sunk as a target in 1996.

(Crown Copyright/MoD)

HMS SOBERTON

Built by Fleetlands Shipyards, Gosport, she was completed in 1957, but it was to be 1958 before she commissioned for service with the FPS. Unlike many of her contemporaries, which switched between squadrons, SOBERTON remained with the FPS throughout her very long career, save for a refit in 1978. She decommissioned in 1992 and was eventually sold for scrap in 1998, being broken up at Bruges, Belgium. *(Crown Copyright/MoD)*

HMS SOUTHAMPTON

Built by Vosper Thornycroft, Woolston and commissioned in 1981. Her career was interrupted in 1988 following a collision with the container ship MV TORBAY. The destroyer was on Armilla Patrol at the time and escorting a convoy through the Straits of Hormuz. She was hit forward causing extensive damage to the bridge and Sea Dart launcher. She was returned to the UK on a heavylift ship and her repairs were combined with a scheduled refit in 1989 which cost £45 million. In 2005, together with RFA GREY ROVER, she successfully intercepted a vessel in the Caribbean carrying cocaine valued at £350 million. She decommissioned in 2009 and was scrapped in Turkey in 2011. *(Crown Copyright/MoD)*

HMS SPARTAN

Built by Vickers and completed in 1979, she was the fifth of the Swiftsure class and the eleventh nuclear-powered attack sub-marine to enter RN service. Compared to the Valiant class she had a tubular pressure hull with a constant diameter over a greater length of the hull. In 1982 she was diverted directly from Exercise Spring Train off Gibraltar, in response to the Ar-gentine invasion of the Falklands and was the first submarine to reach Falkland waters. She returned to the UK after 13 weeks submerged. In 1999, she was fitted with Tomahawk cruise missiles. She was also capable of the covert insertion and recovery of Special Forces personnel via a dry shelter deck. She was decommissioned in 2006. *(Crown Copyright/MoD 1986)*

HMS SPEEDY

A 119-tonne jetfoil that was built by Boeing in Seattle and fitted out by Vospers of Portsmouth with much British equipment aboard. She was ordered in 1978 to evaluate the offshore oil and fishery protection roles and other roles where the RN could use her unique capabilities of high speed and extreme manoeuvrability. Although she achieved success in the FP role, being able to arrive on scene very rapidly, she was limited by weather (unable to operate in sea states above 5) and by endurance (on foils she could only run for ten hours at 45 knots). The ship was withdrawn from service in 1982 and offered for sale. She is seen here prior to having RIBs and Handling davits fitted aft of the bridge. *(Crown Copyright/MoD 1979)*

HMS STRIKER
Built by Fairey Allday Marine, Southampton, and completed in 1983 she was one of three Tracker class, together with ATTACKER and HUNTER, deployed to the Mediterranean to form the Cyprus Squadron where they provided security around the Sovereign Base Areas and conducted anti-terror patrols in the surrounding waters. Unlike the training ships, which were unarmed, these vessels carried three general purpose machine guns. Once decommissioned she was transferred to the Lebanon in 1992 and renamed SAIDA.

(Crown Copyright/MoD 1990)

RFA STROMNESS

One of three ships designed as floating supermarkets, she was built by Swan Hunter, Wallsend, and completed in 1967. She carried 40,000 different items of general naval stores including stocks of clothing, mess gear and medical supplies, together with dry and refrigerated food which enabled the Fleet to remain at sea for considerable periods. She also carried up to 350 tons of potable water. She was destoring in 1982 to pay off, but was rapidly brought back into service to move 429 Royal Marines, stores and ammunition to the South Atlantic. In 1983 she was transfered to the US Military Sealift Command, where she was fitted with a hangar and renamed USNS SATURN. She was sunk as a target in 2010. *(US Navy)*

RFA TIDEPOOL

Built by Hawthorne Leslie and Co Ltd, Newcastle she was completed in 1963, one of a pair of Improved Tide class tankers. These ships incorporated a flightdeck and hangar to operate ASW helicopters. Sold to Chile in 1982, she was "borrowed" back for the Falklands War, sailing to Curacao via the Panama Canal to pick up a UK crew, then proceeding south to support the 'Fearless' group. Following the war she was returned to Chile where she served as ALMI-RANTE GORGE MONTT until decommissioning in 1997.

(Crown Copyright/MoD)

RFA TIDESPRING

The second of the Improved Tide class, and also completed in 1963 by Hawthorne Leslie and Co. Ltd, she found herself in 1982 on Exercise Springtrain - her final operational tasking prior to decommissioning. Again, the Falklands intervened and she sailed south with the Antrim Group and supported the action to retake South Georgia, during which she lost both of her helicopters. Post war she was refitted and received a modern bridge and continued in service until 1991. She was broken up at Alang, India, in 1992.

(Crown Copyright/MoD)

HMS TORQUAY

The last of the Whitby Class Type 12 frigates in service (although EASTBOURNE was still in use as a static Harbour Training Ship at Rosyth), she was built by Harland and Wolff and completed in 1956. She served with the 5th FS in Home waters and the Mediterranean and in 1956 was part of the invasion force at Suez. From 1962-70 she served with the DTS and from 1972-83 she served as a Navigational Training Ship with additional deckhouses built aft. She remained in the training role until 1985 when she paid off, having been replaced by the converted Leander class frigate JUNO.

(Crown Copyright/MoD)

HMS TRAFALGAR

Built by VSEL and completed in 1983 she was the lead boat of the Trafalgar class, a development of the earlier Swiftsure class and very similar in appearance (the T boats could be distinguished by a higher rudder than their predecessors). Equipped with Tigerfish (later Spearfish) torpedoes, Sub-Harpoon (since withdrawn) and TLAM, they are very potent weapon systems and have been called into action on more than one occasion. TRAFALGAR launched TLAM against enemy positions in Afghanistan during Operation Veritas in 2002. She decommissioned in 2009 and is laid up afloat awaiting disposal.

(Crown Copyright/MoD)

HMS TURBULENT

Built by VSEL and completed in 1984 at an estimated cost of £160 million. The internal layout is almost identical to the S boats, and is only 2.5 metres longer. However, at a dived displacement of 5,300 tonnes the Trafalgar class is significantly larger. The design includes a new reactor core and upgraded sonar (originally Type 2020, then replaced by Type 2076). Some of the improvements are aimed at reducing underwater radiated noise, including a pumpjet propulsion system rather than a conventional propeller, and anechoic tiles on the hull. In 2003 TURBULENT launched TLAM against Iraq during Operation Telic. She paid off in 2011, to be replaced by one of the newer Astute class.

(Crown Copyright/MoD

SS UGANDA

A cruise liner operated by the British-India Steam Navigation Company she was requisitioned for duty during the Falklands War as a Hospital Ship. She offloaded her passengers at Naples and entered a three day refit at Gibraltar where she was fitted with a flightdeck, replenishment at sea capability, satellite communications and her wards and operating theatres kitted out. She treated 730 casualties, 150 of them Argentine making four rendezvous with the Argentine hospital ships. She returned to Southampton on 9 August 1982, 113 days after sailing to join the Task Force. In January 1983 she was requisitioned for a further two years as a troop ship sailing between Ascension and the Falklands. *(Crown Copyright/MoD)*

HMS UPTON

Built by J.I. Thornycroft & Co, Southampton, she was completed in 1956 and commissioned for service with the 105th MSS based at Harwich). She took part in the Suez Crisis in 1956 prior to returning to the UK to pay off. From 1957-65 she operated with 100th MSS based at Vernon and saw further service with 2 MCMS and 1 MCMS at Port Edgar and Vernon respectively. In 1975 she transferred to 10th MCMS, Tyne Division RNR where she was renamed NORTHUMBRIA. Following a refit at Gibraltar (1976) she served with 10th, 3rd and 1st MCMS and FPS before paying off in 1990. She was sold in October the following year for breaking up.

(Crown Copyright/MoD)

HMS VALIANT

Built by Vickers and completed in 1966. She was the first all British designed nuclear-powered submarine, substitut-ing the US S5W nuclear plant, used in the earlier DREADNOUGHT, for a British designed system. In 1967 he com-pleted a 28 day submerged transit from Singapore to the UK, at the time, a record for an RN submarine. She saw service in the Falklands War and underwent her third refit in 1989. By 1990 the class were becoming worn out and there were increasing concerns over reliability. In 1994 she was withdrawn from service and remains afloat at Devonport while a decision is made on how to dispose of her.

(Crown Copyright/MoD)

HMS WAKEFUL

Built as the commercial tug HERCULES by Cochranes and completed in 1965 for Swedish owners. She was purchased by the RN in 1974, and renamed WAKEFUL, for use as an FPS vessel until sufficient Island class had entered service. She also conducted counter-terror operations off Northern Ireland with the aim of disrupting arms shipments. Following a refit at Chatham in 1976 she was deployed to the Clyde as a submarine tender and target vessel. She paid off in 1987, being replaced by SENTINEL. She was sold to Hellenic Salvage Tugboats in 1988 and renamed AEGEAN PELAGO.

(Stuart Tarlton)

HMS WARSPITE

She was the second of the pair of Valiant class submarines built by Yarrow and completed in 1967. Together with VALIANT and a pair of Oberon class submarines, she formed the Third Submarine Squadron (SM3) based at Faslane. At the height of the Cold War, the nuclear-powered fleet submarines conducted intelligence and surveillance operations, which, even today are rarely talked about, and few details of which have emerged or been confirmed. WARSPITE was in refit during the Falklands campaign, but did carry out a post war patrol to the region. She decommissioned in 1991 and is in long term storage afloat at Devonport.

(Crown Copyright/MoD)

HMS WAVENEY

One of twelve such vessels, all named after British rivers, built by Richards Shipbuilders, she was complete in 1984. With a traditional steel hull to a design based on a commercial offshore support vessel the ships were intended as EDATS sweepers. Armament comprised a 40mm Bofors gun on a WWII era hand operated mount. The first eleven were operated by the 10th MCMS at Rosyth and assigned to various RNR Divisions. The remaining vessel, BLACKWATER, was operated by the RN. WAVENEY was sold to the Bangladesh Navy in 1994 and renamed BNS SHAPLA. *(Crown Copyright/MoD)*

HMS WILTON

Although looking like the preceeding 116 Ton class vessels, WILTON was built by Vosper Thornycroft, Southampton, completing in 1973. Instead of the traditional wooden hull of the rest of the class, she had a Glass Reinforced Plastic hull, the largest vessel at that time to use such construction. Much of her equipment was taken from the scrapped DERRITON. After a 21 year career she paid off in 1994, but such were the properties of her hull, she survives today as the Club HQ of Essex Sailing Club at Leigh-on-Sea.

(Crown Copyright/MoD 1991)

HMS WOTTON

She was a Dartmouth built vessel, being completed in 1957 by Philip & Son. From 1958-71 she operated as part of the FPS before transferring to 3 MCMS based at Portland during which time she spent several periods operating on counter arms smuggling operations off Northern Ireland. In 1982 during the Falklands War the majority of her crew transferred to FARNELLA (*see page 80*) In April 1984 WOTTON operated with 10th MCMS RNR as London Division Training Ship, but this was to be shortlived as she paid off in November that year. She was scrapped at Bruges in 1992.

(Crown Copyright/MoD)

HMS YARNTON

Completed in 1957 by William Pickersgill & Sons, Sunderland, she was attached to the 100th MSS at Port Edgar. Following a long refit at Chatham in 1966 she deployed to Bahrain as part of the 9th MCMS, deploying to the Far East for refits. In 1971 she was refitted as a patrol craft at Hong Kong for service with the 6th HKPS. She remained with the squadron until paying off in 1984. She was sold to Pounds of Portsmouth in 1986 for disposal, being scrapped locally in Hong Kong.

(Crown Copyright/MoD)

HMS YORK

Built by Swan Hunter and completed in 1985. She is seen here with Phalanx CIWS installed in the boats former position, which are now displaced further aft and served by a crane visible by the hangar. The increase in topweight would see the four Batch III vessels receive hull strengthening beams fitted to the outer hull. In 2003 the ship was involved in operations against Iraq and in 2006 was instrumental in evacuating British national from Beirut during increased tension between Israel and Lebanon. She conducted similar operations in 2011 during the Libyan revolution. By 2012 she was one of only two Type 42s remaining in service.

(Crown Copyright/MoD 1988)

HMS ZULU

A Tribal class general purpose frigate built by Alex Stephen & Sons, Govan, she was completed in 1964. A single shaft design, ZULU was unique among the Tribals in that she was fitted with two quadruple Seacat launchers either side of the mast. She joined 9th FS east of Suez until August 1965 when she returned to the UK. In 1979 she joined the Standby Squadron at Chatham, but was recommissioned in 1982 during the Falklands War to cover for ships lost and damaged. She paid off in 1984 and was transferred to Indonesia, being renamed MARTHA KHRYSTINA TIYAHADU.

(Crown Copyright/MoD)

INDEX